REVIEWS FOR

Victorious

C.S. Lewis once wrote: "Pain insists upon being attended to. God whispers to us in our pleasures, speaks in our consciences, but shouts in our pains. It is his megaphone to rouse a deaf world." *Victorious* not only rehearses the deep pain of the loss of a child, but it also is rich with the delightful attributes of God, which strengthens and calms during such times. This book is hard to put down because it is written as if you are in the room watching each event unfold. I highly recommend this book and trust God's glory will be manifest through it!

Susan Heck: author, speaker, certified counselor. www.withthemaster.org

Katie has written beautifully of a mother's love for her daughter and our Father's love and grace. As you read her story, you will cry with her, rejoice with her, and grow with her. I never met Colette, but through her mother's story I have come to know Colette and Katie and to know even more about the love and grace of our God.

Jeff Walton, executive director, American Association of Christian Schools

It has been said that "you will never find a bundle of affliction that does not have in it somewhere sufficient grace." Katie Piazza has boldly shared her "affliction" and masterfully directed us to the sufficient grace and amazing victory found in Christ! This book is an outstanding resource for all those who have experienced life's deepest pains.

Pastor Rick Dressler, Senior Pastor of Maple City Baptist Church in Chatham, Ontario

"Yea, though I walk through the valley of the shadow..." If you have ever been in this valley, or you are in the valley now, here is a book that will comfort, inspire, and encourage you. It describes the journey of two godly parents, and their precious daughter, whom God sovereignly and lovingly led into the valley of the shadow. As Tim & Katie's pastor, I was privileged to witness firsthand their devotion and love to Christ and heartened to see our God's comforting and sustaining grace to them in such a difficult providence. As with all journeys in the valley, theirs was bitter/sweet. Bitter in that it caused pain and heartache, sweet in that this pain was not wasted. I encourage you to read of their journey, that you might be reassured that through Christ, on the other side of the valley is true victory!

Glenn Dunn
Pastor of Cornerstone Bible Fellowship
Moderator and Board Member of the Fellowship of Independent Reformed Evangelicals
Executive Director of the Biblical Counseling Institute
Certified ACBC Counselor

Victorious

A Mother and Daughter's Journey
Through the Valley of the Shadow

Katie Piazza

Published by KHARIS PUBLISHING, imprint of KHARIS MEDIA LLC.

Copyright © 2020 Katlyn Piazza

ISBN-13: 978-1-946277-69-5
ISBN-10: 1-946277-69-X

Library of Congress Control Number: 2020943667

All KHARIS PUBLISHING products are available at special quantity discounts for bulk purchase for sales promotions, premiums, fund-raising, and educational needs. For details, contact:

Kharis Media LLC
Tel: 1-479-599-8657
support@kharispublishing.com
www.kharispublishing.com

CONTENTS

CHAPTER 1

The Sentencing

There are few children who are born under a death sentence; few who enter the world beneath such a shadow. In a small, darkened room, I read of such a child.

I had heard the story countless times, but now I read it with eyes that hungered— devouring things I had never seen before. It was the Biblical account of Moses: born into a Jewish family in ancient Egypt during a time when all male, Jewish infants were ordered by law to be killed at birth. Moses's life was in jeopardy from his first breath. I knew the story; I was familiar with his plight. But this time as I read, my mind was not centered on Moses but instead drawn to his mother.

I could almost see her in my mind. Desperate to save the life of her condemned child, she appeared before me; her anxious, frenzied mind straining to find a way to spare her child from such a cruel sentencing. I saw her determination mount as she fixated on a plan. I watched her gathering supplies, weaving a basket, covering it with the impermeable substance—stopping momentarily to cast a glance at her sleeping son and stifling her growing agony.

The little basket completed, I beheld her sorrow as she lifted her tiny boy out of his hiding place, feeling the warmth of his body against her own.

Then in anguish, she placed him inside the basket. I saw her carry the little vessel down to the Nile River, numb with determination; I watched her place the basket into the great river and push it out into the current "Oh, God," her heart would cry, "have mercy on my son! Let him live. Let the basket be found by someone more powerful than I...let him live."

How she could turn her back and walk home, I did not yet understand. I would eventually, but not yet. However, *why* she did what she did, I fully understood. She did it in hope. However slim, she saw a chance for her child to live. She could not endure the thought of her child dying without raising her hand in his defense. However unlikely the chance, however reckless her actions may have appeared, she had hope that perhaps God would be merciful. Perhaps God would be gracious. Perhaps through some miracle, her son would be victorious.

I understood this mother. I could see and feel her passions so easily because when I lifted my eyes from the pages, there lay another child who had been born under a death sentence. Before me, in a tiny hospital crib, slept my daughter.

I, too, could not endure the thought of her dying without raising my hand in her defense. I, too, clung to a slim hope that perhaps God would be merciful. Perhaps God would be gracious. Perhaps by the means of some miracle, my daughter would not succumb to her sentence.

"Oh, God," I prayed, "let her live. Let her be victorious."

CHAPTER 2

He Makes My Feet like the Feet of a Deer

G rowing up, I never dreamed I would utter such a prayer. I never imagined such darkness lay before me. From my earliest memories my life seemed to be marked by happiness. How naive to believe nothing but happiness awaited me.

I grew up in a Christian home that was filled with sweetness and love. From my childhood, I learned about God. I was taken to church, sent to a Christian school, and was taught from the Bible at home. It was not long before I not only knew about Jesus, but I knew Him myself. At five years old, I realized I was a sinner in need of a Savior and accepted Jesus' offer of salvation. From that moment on, Jesus Christ became the growing center of my life. The more I knew Him, the more I loved Him. How could I not?

Following graduation from high school, I went to college for nursing. During this time, I began dating and eventually married Tim Piazza, an elementary school teacher, who had attended the same church and Christian school. I finished my degree during our early years of marriage and began working as an emergency department nurse while Tim began his work as the vice principal of a Christian school.

A few months after our second anniversary, we received the happy news that I was expecting. Our son, TJ, was born in October of 2015. It was after his birth that I took a part-time position in the emergency department which allowed me to spend most of my days at home. Life was sweet in the Piazza household, and it looked like nothing but sweetness in the forecast. This leads to my journal entry written a little over a year after TJ's birth:

December 15, 2016, Thursday
Today my cup is full to the brim with joy! God's goodness has reached down once more to earth, filling me with new life! I am pregnant again! What a magnificent Christmas gift. Bless the Lord, O my soul, let all that is within me bless His Holy Name!

This entry is most incredible because it was both legible and understandable…I remember that beautiful day, feeling dizzy with joy. A joy made more exquisite because of a miscarriage two months prior—the first dark cloud that threatened our little kingdom of sunshine. During one of the days in which the miscarriage had not yet been confirmed but appeared to be imminent I wrote:

My hope is almost gone. My head aches from crying…I just keep hearing the words from the hymn "Be Still My Soul,"
"Leave to thy God to order and provide,
In every change He faithful will remain…"
My Father is deciding what is best for our family. Even now, He could save this life. He could intervene. I beg Him to, but I trust His way will be best. I go for an ultrasound and blood work at 1:15.

The next day, my journal holds the words: *There is no more baby.* Up until that point, I had never experienced such pain. While it crept into my life like a sudden unexpected and unwelcome visitor, the reality of God as the great Comforter entered in as well. God's comfort, I have found, is rarely a flashy thing. It is a gentle, quiet reassurance that wears many different disguises. At times, it was the silent presence of a friend, or the words of an old hymn or Bible verse that gracefully flowed through my mind. The days slipped by as my grief and sorrow gave way to hope. On that day in December, when I discovered the glorious news, my heart overflowed with thankful joy.

How grateful I was to once more be counting down the days and weeks until I would meet the source of such perfect happiness. Just how much happiness this baby would bring me, I did not yet imagine; nor could I imagine the great sorrow this child would introduce me to, as well. I did not know, so I danced on, blissfully unaware. The next day, I wrote:

I have managed to keep the glorious news to myself regarding the dear little baby. Tim, I obviously told but everyone else is to be kept in the dark, at least until Christmas. All I want to do is dwell on it…just think and dream of the beauty of it…what bliss!

I remained the creature of this joyful dream until the cruel reality of morning sickness commandeered my life. My first pregnancy had included extensive quality time near toilets and waste-paper baskets, and this pregnancy proved to be a hardy encore of my first performance. My days were filled with caring for our fifteen-month-old son, keeping up with housework and working my few shifts in the emergency department. Looking back, those winter days have a foggy, dim haze over them. In my mind, the finish line in August seemed miles away, and the only reality seemed to be my exhausted, nauseated body. However, spring came, as it always does; for no winter can last forever. With it came the sweet revelation that our baby was to be a little girl! Once more, joy filled every fiber of my being:

April 14, 2017, Friday
It's a GIRL! Miss Colette Diana Piazza is on her way! What a shock we received— I didn't want to dare hope! I've only known for a few hours so I'm still trying to wrap my mind around it—a daughter—a little girl. Oh my darling little girl, how badly I've longed for you—how thankful I am that you are coming!

The summer before Colette's birth was as brilliant and beautiful as the winter had been dreary and dark. It seemed as though God had restored life and energy to me, and though I did not know it at the time, He was actively preparing me for the storm that was still months in the distance. In Psalm 18:33 David speaks of God, "He makes my feet like the feet of a deer, and sets me on my high places." I have always loved that verse as it speaks of God's tender care for His children. Just as He made the hoof of the deer perfectly fitted for the high and rocky slopes, He is ever preparing us for the trials that lie ahead. The summer before Colette's birth was one in which God truly was at work "preparing my feet".

As the nausea and vomiting decreased in my third trimester, I found my times of prayer grew, not surprisingly, much sweeter! I suddenly had the desire to memorize hymns such as "Be Still My Soul" and "How Firm a Foundation." I was also reading through the book of Isaiah with the assistance of a commentary which seemed to open up a whole new world of beauty and hope for the future. I never before realized how much the book of Isaiah speaks of Heaven and the Millennial Kingdom.

The phrase "in that day" (which is sprinkled liberally throughout the book) indicates Christ's Millennial Kingdom, the time when Christ will return and rule over the earth making things perfect once more. I began to think and dream of the reality of "that day" in which there will be no more sorrow, no more trouble. I longed for the day that all hope would be restored, for as C.S. Lewis said, "Joy is the serious business of heaven…"[1]

I snatched up verses from Isaiah to memorize, such as Isaiah 41:10 "Fear not, for I am with you; be not dismayed, for I am your God. I will strengthen you, yes, I will help you, I will uphold you with My righteous right hand"— verses full of courage and reminders of God's everlasting love and presence in our lives. I stored these verses in my mind in preparation for the upcoming labor and delivery. I memorized verses on contentment and God's sovereignty, arming myself to combat those sleepless nights and the weary days that would undoubtedly follow. As an experienced second-time mother, I knew the strain that fatigue brings! Never before had I felt such an urgency to memorize Bible verses, and certainly had I never memorized hymns! But God was at work, quietly and wisely making my feet sure for the days ahead. When the rocky path would lead me to places high and treacherous, my feet would not slip.

One final preparation, it seems, was taking place during those months before Colette's birth. I had always felt a longing to ease suffering. As a nurse, I thrilled at opportunities to mitigate pain and comfort the fearful. However, those days of nursing opened my eyes to a different type of suffering. I saw aches and wounds of the soul which appeared just as troublesome and excruciating at times as those of the body. I saw people in wide-eyed fits of anxiety. I witnessed deep depressions and fears of all kinds. Simple conversations with patients would lead to discussions of their losses, emotional pain, and struggles.

Everyone in the emergency department, it seemed, had internal pain; pain that could not be alleviated by the medications I could administer. Eventually I realized this was not a problem limited to those within the hospital walls; *everyone* has internal pain. My heart longed to bring relief—I wanted to give peace and hope. It was during this time that God directed my path to a church that was teaching the principles of Biblical counseling, an approach to meeting the deep spiritual and soul needs of a person through the use of the Bible alone.

I began taking classes several times a month and later enrolled in their two-year program with the intention of becoming a certified Biblical counselor. These classes were liberating. I learned not only about the beauty

---

[1] From *Letters to Malcolm: Chiefly on Prayer*

of the Bible, I began to learn how to skillfully use it. The teaching transformed my thinking and gave me a new and deep faith in God's Word. I began to believe that the Bible was sufficient for any of life's storms. The teacher of the class, who eventually became my pastor, often told us two things that remained entrenched in my mind during my days in the "high places." The first was, "Let your faith inform your feelings" which led the battle cry for me to trust in things that I did not feel or that did not appear true in the moment. I learned to believe in things because they *were* true not merely because they *felt* true at the time. The second was, "The simplicity of my Bible helps me with the complexity of this life." How true those words became to me. I finished the work required for certification a few weeks before Colette's due date. God's preparation was now complete. It was time for me to be "set" in my high place.

CHAPTER 3

Our Good and Perfect Gift

C olette arrived on August 15, 2017, our good and perfect gift. On the day of her birth, I began a new journal, writing:

My world has been most joyfully transformed today! At 12:14 AM, Colette Diana Piazza entered the world—the sweetest, tiniest angel. I'll have to close soon as she's coming from the nursery any minute, but I just wanted to record this happy day. God has been so good—what a good and perfect gift.

Her delivery had gone smoothly, and following the all clear from her pediatrician, Tim and I took her home to meet her big brother two days later. We quickly settled into our new routine. Tim began his new position as an elementary school principal. His first day of school was actually the day of her birth…I believe Colette enjoyed stealing the show that day.

My world revolved around mastering the art of juggling two little ones under two years old. I believe every mother has her favorite season of mothering. There are those who relish the toddler years or the imagination era that dawns with preschool. I cannot say which season is my favorite, not having traveled down the road of motherhood very far; but I must say, I love the first few weeks with a newborn. I seem to soar on a surge of adrenalin-infused optimism which is shocking, really, when I consider how dearly I value sleep. However, the truth remains: I LOVE my time with my newborns.

My journal entries in the first few weeks of Colette's life reflect this, each cluttered with the all-consuming critical points: feeding times, sleeping times and naturally, utter adoration of my tiny little lady. We checked off the early post-delivery doctor visits which left us more proud of our little girl. She was developing just as she ought and was the sweetest, most content baby one could wish for. On August 31, I wrote about her two week check up saying,

Colette has gained 15 ounces in the past ten days! She is 7 lbs and 15 oz! The doctor said she is gaining beautifully and is in perfect health. So thankful to God for our healthy, beautiful children.

Not even the tiniest of grey clouds had invaded our blue skies; nothing to forewarn of the storm that was building. A week later, I wrote:

September 6, 2017
She is three weeks old today…I still can't believe I have a daughter! Me! I get a little girl AND a little boy…they are my crown jewels; even if they do devise ways to rob me of sleep in the most devious ways. I'm so blessed. Thank you, Father, for such a gift!

At a month old we were tackling various firsts: first trip to the grocery store, which I recorded as "very time consuming…we moved like a pack of snails"; first time at the park; first smile! Our home had slipped into a beautiful rhythm of contented existence. Tim was enjoying his new job, and TJ, Colette, and I were enjoying our little world at home.

September 19, 2017
Another day in our little paradise—to be sure, I never expected so many poopy diapers, rashes, and interrupted nights to be in paradise, but to my surprise it seems they are essential elements! TJ played the morning away while Colette watched and slept at intervals. I cleaned the dining room and decorated for fall…

September 29, 2017
Such a beautiful day in so many ways! First of all, my children are the sweetest morsels of life—to be nursing Colette and have TJ bound into the room with his giant dark brown eyes wide with earnestness and babble for a minute straight without using one intelligible word—sheer bliss! Colette is looking more beautiful every day, and TJ is learning

by leaps and bounds. He loves Colette. He loves checking on her, fetching her pacifier, and piling "blankies" on her. We played outside this morning in the gloriously crisp fall weather…

Now, if these entries seem a bit unrealistically buoyant, I defend myself in three ways. The first as previously mentioned—I love the early days with a newborn and seem to float along for the first couple months on sheer adrenaline alone. My second defense is my absolute love of fall. Like many a parched plant, I perk up in the cooler weather. My final defense is that I am typically an unrealistically buoyant person! I certainly do have my down days, but they are few and far between; I have a positive aversion to sadness.

With the advent of October, came more sweet moments along with the following eerily prophetic entry:

October 9, 2017, Monday

A lovely, cozy, rainy day…Colette is asleep upstairs, and I hear the repeating phrase "Choo! Choo!" echoing from the sun room as TJ and Flossie [his favorite stuffed rabbit that was his ever-faithful companion] *play trains and cars and all things with wheels. Life is so sweet. I know one day I'll look back at these journal entries, and after laughing at the misspellings, I will cry for the beautiful days that were. But oh, I am enjoying them. I'm clinging to the experiences—the warmth of the little ones, the smell of their little heads after bath time, the sweetness and purity of our little kingdom here at Meadowbrook.*

Picture: Our good and perfect gift

On October 16th, Colette went for her two-month check-up where she received a glowing bill of health. She was growing and gaining weight;

her four-month appointment was made, and I once again thanked God for a healthy daughter. As the month drew on, I began making preparations for TJ's second birthday. His party was scheduled for Saturday, October 28, but on Tuesday there was a change in our sweet, even-tempered Colette. The dark clouds were beginning to gather.

October 24, 2017, Tuesday

Fall has come, I believe—today has been a cool, rainy day with little periods of sunshine that makes it feel ever so cozy! Colette had a difficult night—she gets so worked up! She wakes and cries and won't be comforted. Over and over this happens until finally she seems to calm down and drifts off to sleep.

The following day I wrote:

October 25, 2017, Wednesday

It's never a good night when you find yourself sobbing in unison with your baby. Colette is still out of sorts. All day yesterday she was clingy and fussy. It continued throughout the night. She was up about every two hours and then it took about an hour to two hours to get her back down. By six in the morning I was sobbing myself. I just felt so helpless and hopeless! For some reason, I can never see the big picture at night.

CHAPTER 4

The High Place

There was no party for TJ that Saturday. The storm had broken and God had set me in the high place.

At this point, I will allow my journal entries to tell the story—Colette's story, our story, but ultimately God's story. I will interject as needed for clarity sake, but I believe the best avenue for sharing the truth of those days will come from the pages I wrote in the midst of the storm, when the darkness surrounded, and we truly learned what it meant to "walk by faith, not by sight" (2 Cor 5:7).

November 5, 2017, Sunday

Oh, what a change one week has made in our home—our beautiful, cozy life of sweet routine has been shaken to the core, and we are all tossed into a world of foggy uncertainty. I last wrote on Wednesday, and it may take me some time to catch up, but this journey must be recorded.

That Wednesday night proved to be another difficult night, although I seemed to be more resigned to sleeplessness. I was nearly hourly with Colette as she seemed only to be able to sleep when I was holding her. In the morning, Colette seemed to improve and slept well throughout the day. However, she grew fussy again in the evening and began refusing to eat. She had no fever and was still making wet diapers. Still, I watched carefully for any sign of dehydration. On Thursday night, she began to periodically vomit, I called the pediatrician and was told to make her an appointment first thing in the morning. I called at 8:00 AM sharp and had her scheduled for 9:15.

When I laid her down to change her diaper before leaving, her back arched, and she gave me the scariest startled look that instantly made me think of an image I'd seen in a nursing textbook of "sunset" eyes—a sign of hydrocephalus. I told Tim that I didn't like that and shot off for the doctor's office. She repeated the look again when I laid her down to be weighed. The pediatrician examined her and he agreed that she looked dehydrated, although he was puzzled as to why. She had no fever and no cough or congestion. He said he wasn't too concerned about the look—he believed it could be due to increased irritability from being sick. He told me her fontanelles were soft², and he ordered blood work and a urine culture. I took her over to the lab center where she got a heel-stick for the blood samples and then had to be straight catheterized for the urine sample. No urinary tract infection was seen; and, aside from elevated platelets, her blood work only showed mild dehydration. During all this waiting time, she slept and I called my mom. I told her to look up hydrocephalus. I told her it looks just like that, except it can't be that "because that's serious and rare…but it looks like it." The doctor then sent us to the adjoining emergency department for rehydration and further evaluation. By this point, I cancelled TJ's birthday party and began to worry.

I called Tim and TJ to give them an update and then called my mom to come provide back up—as I was exhausted and starving from a week of sleepless nights and not eating all day. The physician's assistant that first examined Colette in the emergency department immediately called for the attending doctor who promptly suggested that Colette be transferred to Rainbow³ downtown. The doctor was not comfortable with the arch that Colette would do if laid down particularly as, at this point, Colette's eyes were beginning to deviate, looking exclusively to the right. Colette began to alternate between periods of inconsolable crying and sleeping. The emergency room doctor wanted her to be evaluated by a neurologist. She said, at the best, it may just be acid reflux and at the worst, seizures. Either way, she needed further evaluation. I signed all the papers for the transfer. After which, Colette got an IV and a bolus of fluids. My mom, who had been driving to the emergency room where we were, then headed to Rainbow to meet us, as we were told her transfer would occur quickly.

Things went downhill from there. Colette's IV infiltrated [dislodged from her vein resulting in the fluid going into the surrounding tissue making her arm swollen and painful] *and needed to be removed. The staff did not want to replace it as "she could just get another one at Rainbow." Then I was told that there were no available beds at Rainbow; so while my mom sat waiting downtown, we sat at the emergency room*

² Fontanelles are areas in a baby's skull that are not covered by the cranium. They are typically soft. Hard fontanelles indicate that there is a build up of pressure in the brain; sunken fontanelles are a sign of dehydration

³ University Hospital's Rainbow Babies and Children's Hospital is a children's hospital located in downtown Cleveland, Ohio about a half-hour from our home.

thirty minutes away…for seven hours. A couple of hours in, I asked for another IV to be placed and another bolus given (as Colette continued not to eat). I also requested something for her pain as she was clearly suffering.

At 8:30 PM, the ambulance arrived and we finally set off for Rainbow—direct admission to a medical surgical floor. Tim and my mom met us there. We all went up to her room—a shared room with a noisy, large family who apparently considered yelling at their children therapeutic. For a few terrible minutes I thought, "I can't do this—I can't handle this!" God must have mercifully agreed and sent an angel of a nurse to take pity on us. After examining Colette, she found us another room.

The resident doctor and the attending doctor were extremely thorough in their exams. They thought Colette's right side was a little weaker than her left side; and after asking many questions, they suggested a CT scan. The attending said, "In the end, I hope this ends up being a case of 'Much Ado About Nothing,' but I want to be safe—there are just too many odd things that I want to look further." So down to CT we went, Colette in my arms as I was pushed, per protocol, in a wheelchair. After the scan, my mom rocked her to sleep; Tim and I collapsed on the sofa in the room.

I woke to see the resident doctor, a young girl with a soft, gentle voice dressed in a purple and black plaid shirt, jeans, and tennis shoes sitting across from us. We sat up, and as I searched for my glasses, I heard her say, "Mom and Dad, I have some not so good news for you—her CT scans showed a mass in the back of the left portion of her brain…" She went on to explain that it was causing a back up of cerebrospinal fluid [the fluid that surrounds the brain and the spinal cord] *resulting in Colette's symptoms. The mass was either a tumor or a cyst—they needed to do an MRI to know more. All the while I felt frozen—mouth open, dry-eyed frozen. The thought that kept spinning over and over in my mind was "This is so strange—I need to focus" and yet I couldn't—I couldn't think, and I certainly didn't comprehend what it all meant. I just felt dazed and shocked.*

It was a hustle after that—Tim and I crying and hugging, yet still not understanding. The nurses and doctors descended, examining her and preparing her to be transferred to the PICU [Pediatric Intensive Care Unit]. *We followed in mute wonder, listening to the next steps with dumbfounded compliance. Before we knew it, Colette had an EVD,* [external ventricular drain which allowed the cerebral spinal fluid which had been trapped in her head by the mass to drain freely, alleviating Colette's pressure and pain] *was sedated, and placed on a ventilator* [a machine used to control and assist breathing; while under sedation, Colette could not breathe on her own]. *She was being prepared for the MRI scan. This all took place early Saturday*

15

morning. We met doctors—neurologists, PICU intensivists, and our new hero, Dr. Tomei, the neurosurgeon.

The MRI showed the mass to be a tumor, specifically, one tumor about 4 cm (size of a walnut) in the left cerebellar region [back of the brain]. *Surgery would be done on Tuesday morning when the most experienced staff would be present, as it would require the top level of care according to Dr. Tomei. Until then, we had to wait and watch Colette decline.*

After the MRI she was able to come off the sedation and be taken off the ventilator. However, she lost head control and required greater and greater amounts of respiratory support as the tumor was pressing on the brain stem causing irregular breathing. It was torture—the fear and the pain. Holding her…with all the wires and tubes was heart-wrenching. One night I was alone with her and held her for about two hours, just drenching her with tears, and yet it was not unbearable. There were moments of great peace and joy and even gratitude. God has entrusted us with this trial—He has chosen us for this special journey. It is a painful honor to be thought worthy.

Monday was TJ's birthday so we went home to be with him for the afternoon while my parents stayed with Colette. We celebrated what I hope will be the most grim birthday of his existence. Kayla [my sister] *and McLaine* [my cousin and also a nurse] *came over bringing joy and a birthday spirit with them. They watched him that night as Tim and I returned to the hospital. That same night Tim, my mom, and I sat through the longest most difficult night of our lives—it felt as though the morning would never come.*

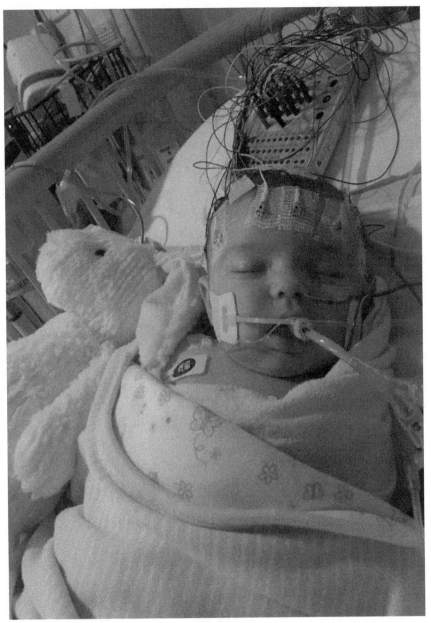

Picture: Waiting for surgery, what a change one week can make

November 6, 2017, Monday

Throughout the night, Colette's breathing was horrible. She had the most strenuous seesaw respirations [movements of the chest that occur naturally when the body is starving for air; it is the body's attempt to suck in and hold more air]. *At one point I went to the nurse privately with tears in my eyes asking if I should be ready for the fact that she might not make it till the surgery. I was terrified. They closely monitored her breathing and eventually got it under control. What a horrible night. I held her, and the tears and prayers were countless.*

In the morning, our pastor, my dad, and Tim's parents arrived for a final prayer. The OR team then arrived to take her away. When I put her in the crib for the last time, I felt much like Abraham must have felt laying Isaac on the altar [Gen. 22]. *I whispered to her Joshua 1:9*

"Have I not commanded you? Be strong and of good courage; do not be afraid, nor be dismayed, for the Lord your God is with you wherever you go."

The peace I had was truly of God—what grace—what goodness of God! It was incredible. I had no tears and oddly enough, no fears. I had only an overwhelming numbness. I couldn't even worry. We were allowed to follow behind her crib up to a certain point. When we were told that we could go no further, we watched her being wheeled away, and I kept thinking that angels were continuing to walk beside her crib—guarding her. She was certainly not alone. My Father would go with her.

Tim and I prayed in the chapel, and all I can say is "the peace that passes all understanding" is a very real thing that truly can be relied on.

"And the peace of God, which surpasses all understanding, will guard your hearts and minds through Christ Jesus" [Philipians 4:7]

The surgery itself did not start until 11:00 AM, then went on for eight and a half hours. We spent the day mastering the art of distraction. Kayla and Lyssa [my sister-in-law] *came to help pass the time, and we lived from update to update from the operating room. Each update was brief, simply letting us know that all was well.*

She came back to us late that night. The joy we felt when Dr. Tomei told us that Colette had done very well was indescribable. She had lost less blood than expected, and

18

the MRI later that night showed no signs of stroke, which had been the two biggest threats. However, Dr. Tomei was not able to remove all of the tumor, which means that a second surgery will be needed. They want to give her a week of recovery before attempting again.

When Colette returned to the room she was under medical paralysis to keep her from moving with the hopes of preventing any intracranial bleeding, and she was intubated on a ventilator. But she—our sweet eleven-week-old baby—had been returned to us! Praise our mighty, good Father! Her recovery was amazing. She remained on a ventilator for several days and was eventually taken off. Every day she improved.

This brings us to today. She is currently being taken down for an MRI to determine how much tumor remains in her brain which will give Dr. Tomei an idea of what tomorrow's surgery will require. However, Colette is breathing on her own and is even sucking her pacifier again. Except for her EVD, femoral line [line into her femoral artery for drawing blood samples and blood pressure monitoring], *and NG* [nasogastric tube—a tube that went through her nose into her stomach through which she could receive breast milk for her nutritional needs], *she seems like our little baby again!*

Tomorrow's surgery is scheduled around 1:00 PM. In the meantime, we wait for the pathology report to see what the beast will be named. We still do not know if it is cancerous or not.

Off to take a walk around Wade Pond [a large pond located just outside the hospital which was to become my retreat during our many days at Rainbow].

The news about Colette spread quickly. By this point, our family was flooded with love from all we knew and many we did not. Colette's room was littered with cards, stuffed animals and treats of all kinds. It is difficult to explain how much it lifts one's spirits to look around and see the evidence of so much love. The gratitude was greater because we knew each token of love linked us to a family member or friend who had begun and would continue to pray for us. We knew our daughter's name was being passed from church to church, from believer to believer, and that an army was forming around us that would not leave our sides. Together through prayer; we ran to the God of Heaven Who is never indifferent to the troubles of His children. What joy there is in the love of the body of Christ.

19

November 8, 2017, Wednesday

It is amazing how comfortable we've become with fear; another major brain surgery down! It's hard to find the words to describe how it feels—to have incredibly skilled professionals swarm the crib side of your twelve-week-old baby, to see them working—buzzing around her like bees each with a separate task—to see her as I do now like a tiny, sleeping doll in a crib surrounded by more wires and tubes than can be imagined, to see all of this without melting into tears. I know two things: God's peace is real, and the human ability to adjust is an amazing thing. I scribble "brain surgery" off of my to-do list just as calmly as I used to scribble off "clean the bathroom." Our life has totally been transformed, and yet we, the people of our life, are still the same. I feel like I've been plucked out of my world and transplanted into a parallel universe. The old world is gone, but all the people I knew in it have joined me here in this new world.

She was taken to surgery around 3:00 PM and returned a little after 11:00 PM. She did very well they tell me. Dr. Tomei felt confident that she was able to remove all the tumor that had remained from the first surgery (this will be confirmed by the MRI which she will soon leave for). She required only a minimal amount of blood (she lost 150 mL) and actually came back from the surgery with her eyes open looking around! She was receiving sedation and pain medication, but apparently the sedation was not strong enough! Dr. Tomei and the team kept laughing because she just laid there calm, with her giant, beautiful eyes peering at us as if to say, "It takes more than a seven-hour brain surgery to knock me out!" It is so Colette—our quiet, calm, incredibly strong baby girl. She is quite the fighter.

She has been intubated and on a ventilator since the surgery. The plan is to extubate once she returns from the MRI today. I'll probably go for a walk and pray while she's getting her MRI.

The MRI came back clear. Having succeeded in removing any visible sign of tumor, the next step would be to attempt to remove the EVD that had been assisting with the removal of cerebrospinal fluid. Now that the tumor was no longer blocking the natural drainage route, the EVD would hopefully no longer be needed.

We were also still waiting for the pathology report which would reveal what type of tumor she had. Before Colette's first surgery, the question was always: is the tumor cancerous or benign? After the surgery, due to some findings during the surgery itself, the question gradually became what type of cancer was the tumor. I say gradually because that was how we were told. It was never a firm, blunt statement, but merely gentle phrases that eventually eased us into the inevitable understanding that the tumor was cancerous. At first the neuro-oncologist, Dr. Stearns, the gentlest and kindest of doctors, would say things like, "It looks as if it is a cancerous tumor…" and "The report will most likely reveal the tumor to be cancerous…"; as the days slipped by, the phrases shifted into "depending on what type of cancer it is…" and "we will know more once we know what type of cancer it is." Without knowing when it happened, Tim and I drifted into the acceptance that Colette's tumor was cancerous, and we were simply waiting to know what type of cancer and what could be done for her.

November 9, 2017, Thursday

I went home yesterday to be with TJ while Tim spent the night with Colette. They apparently had a rough night trying to get her pain medicine on a good schedule. She seems much better now. Today has been all the more special as I was able to nurse her! It's the first time since before the original surgery, and she did wonderful!

PS: She got a fever but the cultures came back negative [no sign of blood stream infection]. *They put her on antibiotics just in case, but they believe the fever is just post-op related.*

November 10, 2017, Friday

My mom and I stayed with Colette last night. We gave her a bath and I was able to nurse her again. She seemed to be uncomfortable until around midnight, but then she slept beautifully! Her temperature was still slightly up today; however the doctors continue to believe (as it is trending down) that it is merely a post-op fever. Still, she is getting her antibiotics and the infectious disease doctor has examined her. They are talking about possibly clamping her EVD soon. Neurosurgery will tell us more later today.

For me, the high points are that I keep getting to hold and nurse her! She really is doing so well.

PS: Tim's with TJ…play day!

November 11, 2017, Saturday

Colette has smiled! It is just amazing to see her returning to us. She is eating well, sleeping well, and now we have a smile! Her chest x-ray and urine culture came back negative for signs of infection. However, she still has a slight fever which is puzzling; she remains on her antibiotic. Also, they have slowly started the process of clamping the EVD. On Monday, they want to clamp it completely and see how she does.

Victorious

November 16, 2017, Thursday

The days have gotten away from me—it is difficult to write now because when she is up, I'm holding her; and when she's asleep, I'm trying to catch up on a million things! However, she is doing so very well. She had her EVD clamped on Monday and removed on Tuesday. She hasn't had a bit of trouble without it. It is so much easier to hold and cuddle her now.

Yesterday evening, we moved to Mac 611 (the oncology floor). At first we were put in an itty-bitty room, but since (thanks to Tim's request) have been moved to a massive two room / one bathroom area with a cot and a rocking chair! The staff also got Colette a bouncy chair that she seems to love. She's smiling and cooing—and no more fever!

Dr. Stearns has told us over and over again that it is amazing how good she looks—no one would ever know she has had two major brain surgeries in two weeks. To quote him "she hasn't skipped a beat!" He said that he can't stress enough how important that is. The pathology results should be finalized today from St. Jude's and Dr. Stearns will take it before the hospital's tumor board to pool all the knowledge for a treatment plan. On Monday, he told us that he believes it is either a medulloblastoma or PNET—both are aggressive brain tumors. Medulloblastomas have a 60% chance of a full recovery and PNET have only a 40% chance. Tim and I had a long cry that night. He also spoke to us about the potential treatment plan: three rounds of a strong chemotherapy regimen followed by three more rounds of an even stronger regimen. There is a risk of fatality during treatment due to infections or liver failure. Long term side effects include hearing loss (which he says is a guarantee, but he could not say to what level), infertility, and increased risk of leukemia later in life. All these risks, and I just cling to the hope that there IS hope. In the meeting I had one question on my mind. I didn't care in what form she would be in when this is over; I just wanted to know: would I have her? Was there a chance? But I couldn't get the words out—Oh, God, let her live!

Every day she grows more endearing; she's like a tumor herself—taking over my heart and mind...and everyone else's it seems! There are thousands of people praying for her. I am so thankful.

I'm currently waiting for the daily rounds [every day "rounds" were done on each patient outside the patient's room in which the patient's condition, test results, goals and concerns were discussed. Family was always welcome to attend]. *Tomorrow, Colette goes to the OR for a Broviac placement* [A central line that would replace the need for an IV. It is a catheter that goes through the chest into the heart and can be left in place for months at a time. It would be required for giving medication, blood products, and fluid, as well as for taking blood samples; however, it was a constant risk of infection].

My journal entries do not indicate when we got the pathology report back. They had been sent several places, but each time they returned inconclusive. Dr. Stearns eventually told us that Colette's tumor could not be identified. It could not be placed in any known category. Although he told us it was more like a PNET brain tumor than any other, he said it would have to be placed in an "other" category—a category that perhaps in the future, with more research, would be identified but until then would remain a mystery. All he knew was that it was extremely aggressive, meaning that it grew rapidly. What it would do in the future, how and if it would spread and how it could be treated were unanswerable questions. To me it meant one thing: God alone knew what we were dealing with—it was to Him I prayed, to Him I pleaded, and it was in Him I hoped. Her chances were (as I knew they would always be) 50/50. God would either heal her or He would not. He alone knew what would be best. These were the truths I used to battle every crushed and broken emotion that coursed through my body during these early days.

The treatment suggested by Dr. Stearns was three rounds (about a month long each) of "induction chemotherapy" which he described to us as being a combination of extremely powerful chemotherapy medications. Colette would need to be hospitalized for the majority of each round, as she would need to be closely monitored for the need of blood transfusions and infections. However, at the end of each round, Dr. Stearns hoped we would be able to spend a few days to a week at home. After the induction chemotherapy rounds, Colette would begin three more rounds of chemotherapy medications that were so strong that they would destroy all her bone marrow, requiring a relatively new procedure called a "rescue stem cell transplant." Colette's stem cells (immature blood cells that could mature into any type of blood product) would be collected through an intricate procedure while she was sedated for several days in the PICU. The collected stem cells would then be stored and given back to her after each round of chemotherapy. It is called a "rescue" transplant because if it were not to occur, Colette's bone marrow would not be able to recover from the chemotherapy, and she would die from infection. This was the slim rope we were offered to hold on to as a chance for a complete recovery. As slim as it was, we rejoiced and reached for it, full of hope that through this treatment, Colette would be victorious.

Victorious

November 18, 2017, Saturday

Yesterday, Colette had her Broviac placed and the central line going into her femoral artery was removed. It was another minor surgery, but still required anesthesia and still made my heart sink when they took her away. They told us she would be groggy when she came out, but of course our gentle warrior came out wide-eyed and sweet as ever. The surgeon said she did wonderful, and the new line works perfectly.

Pastor Dunn visited with us while she was in the OR. We are so thankful for the counsel, prayers, and practical help he gives. In the evening, my parents came to spend the weekend with Colette while Tim and I went home to be with TJ. We very much looked forward to that time. TJ was so sweet! We cuddled, wrestled, and played all Friday evening; but in the middle of the night, TJ woke up crying. The poor guy was sick—coughing and congested. I held and rocked him for an hour, but then grew afraid of taking his germs with me back to Colette or getting sick myself and not being able to be with Colette during her first round of chemotherapy. TJ was still wanting to snuggle, so I swapped places with Tim and let him rock TJ while I had a little cry in my bed.

In the morning, I went to Colette while Tim and TJ had a lazy and cozy day at home. I can't help feeling that my little family is torn apart, and the ache to draw us back together is terrible at times—especially on the drives to and from the hospital. But I remind myself of the verses I memorized before Colette was born—I have learned to be content.

"Not that I speak in regard to need, for I have learned in whatever state I am, to be content: I know how to be abased, and I know how to abound. Everywhere and in all things I have learned both to be full and to be hungry, both to abound and to suffer need. I can do all things through Christ who strengthens me." [Philippians 4: 11-13]

This is what my Father has chosen for me in this season, I <u>will be</u> content.

Colette is doing so wonderful—she smiles and coos, and kicks her little feet. She is even starting to grab at things! Our nights are just like at home except I've added vital sign checks [checking heart rate, respiratory rate, temperature, blood pressure and oxygen saturation levels] *with every feeding. She will start chemotherapy on Monday and we will "take the adventure that Aslan sends us!"[4]*

---

[4] Reference to *The Last Battle* by C.S. Lewis

November 19, 2017, Sunday

Last night after Colette's 3:00 AM feeding, I felt so much fear…such sadness. It was crushing and so very dark. I was so afraid of what the future would be, and I was so afraid to <u>think</u> because I was afraid of where each thought would lead. I feared it would lead to something so painful I couldn't bear.

In the morning, I opened my phone to the "verse of the day", and it read: "Do not remember the former things, nor consider the things of old. Behold, I will do a new thing, now it shall spring forth. Shall you not know it? I will even make a road in the wilderness and rivers in the desert." Isaiah 43:18-19.

My Father is so good—He loves <u>me</u>. He sees and considers me. I am not alone— He is a "very present help in trouble" [Psalm 46:1].

PS: TJ is feeling better

Later

As the day went on, I began to feel sick—sore throat and throbbing head. I went home while my mom and dad stayed with Colette. This seems so wrong—how can I not be there for Colette on her first day of chemo? But how could I stay knowing I'm putting her at risk? I can't imagine why God has done this, but He has. His reasons must be good and wise. Though I don't understand, I must trust Him…but I feel like a terrible Mom, and it hurts.

PS: Mom says that they haven't started the chemo yet and Colette is doing perfectly. She even took a bottle, which is a first.

CHAPTER 5

The First Round

N*ovember 20, 2017, Monday*   *1.1* [Round 1 Day 1]
Colette still hasn't begun her chemo yet. Dr. Stearns first wants her hearing to be tested to establish her baseline hearing prior to chemotherapy which will allow them to monitor her hearing loss.

TJ seems to be doing much better—Tim and he are at the zoo this morning while I'm at home drinking tea and trying to get better. I want to be there so badly to relieve my mom and to hold my little Colette. I need to get better.

November 21, 2017, Tuesday   *1.2*
I am back installed as the nurse/mom of Mac 6011. Her hearing screen is done, and she is on day two of chemotherapy. The hearing test came back perfect. At the moment, she is doing great.

November 23, 2017, Thursday   *Thanksgiving 1.4*

Happy Thanksgiving! My mom and I woke up this morning here at Mac 6011 thankful to have a sweet little Colette to love and enjoy. It matters not that she must be followed around by an IV pole and Foley catheter ⁵bag…she is smiling and so are we!

Tim and TJ came early, and we were together as a family for the first time in twenty-eight days. That was something to be thankful for! TJ marched right up to his sister shouting, "Hi, Coco!" He followed it up with several, "Ahhh…Coco." He wanted to get his (presumably) germy hands on her, but we kept her at a safe distance. I was so thankful that he remembered her! We then left Oma [my mom] *and Colette (with Poppa* [my dad] *on the way), and went to see the family for a quick turkey dinner. Then, while TJ got transferred to the care of Poppa, Tim and I went back to the hospital to spend the evening with our sweet little Colette.*

Oh God, thank You, thank You for being Who You are, letting me know You, and for this sweet, wonderful family You gave me!

---

⁵ A Foley catheter is a rubber tube that goes into the bladder to drain urine. It prevented the urine (containing chemotherapy waste) from coming in contact with and damaging Colette's skin. She was required to have one for the first three days of each round of chemotherapy.

Picture: Happy Thanksgiving! Our first time together as a family since Colette's diagnosis.

November 24, 2017, Friday   *1.5*

    Colette continues to do so well. Tim and I spent the night with her. She did have a little period of nausea and vomiting[6], but other than that, she was an angel. She is so sweet—so many smiles and coos! The PT [Physical Therapist; during the course of Colette's treatments she was followed by a physical therapist (PT) who worked on developmental skills such as head control, rolling over, muscle tone etc. and an occupational therapist (OT) who worked on Colette's eating and drinking which became a progressively greater challenge] *was so pleased with her progress—she is doing so much better with head control. Colette really is incredible, quietly tackling one obstacle at a time. xoxoxoxo*

    Tonight, McLaine is joining me, and tomorrow I'll go home to be with Tim and TJ!

November 25, 2017, Saturday   *1.6*

    Colette seems to be doing better. She gets a little fidgety around feeding time and needs some Zofran for nausea, but we have begun giving most of her feeds through the NG and slowing the rate which seems to help. I will be going home today while Kayla and my mom stay with Colette. Finally sleeping time! Four nights in a row here can really drain you!

November 26, 2017, Sunday   *1.7*

    Today was filled with "treasures of darkness" [referring to Isaiah 45:3 "I will give you the treasures of darkness and hidden riches of secret places, that you may know that I, the Lord, Who call you by your name, am the God of Israel."] *After getting the first night of solid sleep in ages, Kayla and I went to church—my first time back since having Colette! It was wonderful to be back, to be filled again. After church, I got to surprise TJ by getting him up from his nap…oh, to hear him say, "Momma!" We played and played…bubbles, wrestling and dance time! He loved dancing to the Nutcracker—he kept calling out "music! music!" I just drink him in on my days home.*

    As for Colette…she is laughing! My mom got her to laugh for the first time today—bliss!

---

[6] As we begin this period of Colette's journey, it is necessary to describe what a "little period of nausea and vomiting" entailed. You must remember, Colette was a baby. She gave no warning before vomiting, and these episodes were certainly no mere "spit up, wipe the chin with a bib" situations. More often than not, each time she vomited meant that she would need a bath, outfit change and a bedding/blanket change (or the washing of the cloth lining of whatever chair, swing, little seat she was currently nesting in.) This was done day and night; our laundry piles growing higher as Colette's tolerance for feeds grew lower. As you will see in the pages ahead, vomiting became a normal pattern of living for our little girl. A normal that was anything but normal.

November 27, 2017, Monday   *1.8*

Today, I rejoined Colette. She had a rough night with Mom—several vomiting episodes overnight and another one this morning. She has a little cough as well which I'm praying won't turn into anything (the doctors aren't too concerned). Apparently now until Monday is the greatest risk period for infection. Her immune system is at its lowest. If we make it through without any difficulty, we may be able to go home next week. I just started getting a little flicker of hope. I'm fighting tears thinking about it right now—oh, to bring her home! Oh, God please heal her—please let me watch her grow and blossom and glorify You for years and years.

November 30, 2017, Thursday   *1.11*

Colette brings smiles to all who meet her. She hasn't vomited or required any nausea medications for the last twenty-four hours and has even gained weight! We are still waiting for her counts to come up[7]; but once they do, we should be able to go home. I'm getting so excited.

As for TJ, he's doing so well. I got to spend yesterday evening and this morning with him. When I walked in the door, the first thing he said was "music?" then led me up to his room where we put on the Nutcracker and broke out our dancing shoes. I love that sweet, curly-headed darling.

December 2, 2017, Saturday   *1.13*

Colette had a difficult day yesterday. She was increasingly irritable, and her temperature seemed to be creeping up with every vital sign check. She was certainly not her peaceful self. At around 9:00 PM, the doctor agreed that something was different and ordered cultures and some antibiotics. At 2:00 AM she had a fever and vomited twice.

Today she has been irritable off and on, depending on if she has her oxycodone for pain or not, but the fever is gone. I came home to be with the boys while my parents stayed with her tonight.

---

[7] Following chemotherapy, the bone marrow (which makes red blood cells, white blood cells and platelets) is damaged resulting in a drop in the number of blood cells and platelets in the body. Without the normal number of blood cells and platelets, a patient is at risk of infection, shortness of breath, and bleeding. Once the bone marrow begins to recover, the number of blood cells and platelets in the body begin to rise and the patient is at less risk. For Colette, daily lab work was done to determine if transfusions of blood cells or platelets were needed and to determine when Colette's bone marrow was recovered enough for her to go home.

December 4, 2017, Monday   *1.15*

   Colette continues to be not quite herself. She has had periodic fevers and continues to require oxycodone for pain as well as antibiotics. She also had to get a transfusion of red blood cells and platelets yesterday. Still, we do get little bursts of smiles from her, which is wonderful!

   My mommy-tank is full as I've been able to have sweet moments with both TJ and Colette in the past couple of days. Last night, Tim and I took TJ to the playground for some romping; then we went to the store to find Colette a stocking and a few other Christmas treasures. We also bought a new Christmas tree! This came about as I got an electric shock from our old tree while trying to "fluff" out the branches—the poor old thing was struggling this year! The new tree is beautiful! I decorated it after putting TJ down for bed. Our home certainly looks festive now.

   This morning I switched with my mom and resumed care of Colette. Sweet, sweet moments—rocking her to sleep and singing her songs of Jesus. I can't help but think—I want her to know Him, to hear of my good Father, to hear of Heaven. I want to let her know that whatever is coming, she need not be afraid. He has "gone to prepare a place" [John 14:2], and it is a good place. There is nothing to fear.

   She is beautiful—asleep and covered in soft pink. Her little tutu covers her Broviac perfectly.

   Thank you, Father, for this perfect gift!

December 5, 2017, Tuesday   *1.16*

   Today was just an all-around discouraging day. I just feel filled with low-grade stress. I'd love to just cry and sleep! Colette's counts have been slow in rising. Her ANC is 0.08, and she can't go home until it is 1.0.[8] She just seems so uncomfortable, and there's so little I can do for her.

---

[8] The ANC or absolute neutrophil count is one of the numbers that is of particular interest to those on chemotherapy because it indicates how well the immune system is functioning. Normal levels are between 1.5-8.0. Colette had to stay in the hospital until her ANC was above 1.0. Anything less than that left her too vulnerable to be outside the hospital setting.

December 7, 2017, Thursday   *1.17*

    "Wonder of wonders, miracles of miracles!"[9] *We are home! Yesterday morning at rounds we got word that her ANC jumped from 0.08 to 0.42. Suddenly there was a mad dash to declare her fit for discharge. Even though her counts fell short of the 1.0 mark, the rapid trend up meant that she would hit her goal in the next day or so. Her fevers had subsided so there was nothing keeping us from leaving. We packed up the room while Tim, Grandma and Abby* [my Grandma and yet another wonderful cousin] *feverishly purified the house of any and all germs!*

    We left the hospital around 6:00 PM. I couldn't stop watching Colette, who just kept her beautiful eyes wide open as if to drink in the "new world" outside her hospital room. She took it all in as calmly as ever. Bursting with thankfulness to God, I drove her home while the sweet sound of Christmas carols filled our car.

    When we got home, Tim and my mom went to work setting things up while I snuggled Colette in the living room. She seemed to love the lights on the Christmas tree and just stared at them, mesmerized. After getting her evening feeds set up and medicines drawn [Colette received feeds and medicines through the night that went through her NG tube; this began as a remedy for the fact that she could not eat enough during the day due to the nausea and vomiting associated with chemotherapy], *I put her down to sleep…IN HER OWN NURSERY! The princess had returned to her kingdom.*

    It was a difficult night simply because I was trying to mentally juggle all the new information, and she vomited once around 5:30 AM. However, we made it!

December 9, 2017, Saturday   *1.19*

    Colette struggles to sleep at night. She wakes about every 1 ½ to 2 hours, which leaves me exhausted and discouraged in the morning. Still, it has been wonderful to all be under the same roof! And now that I have had a nap, I feel much less hopeless! It is incredible what sleep can do!

    I'm thinking that perhaps she is getting too much food overnight through her NG, and she's waking because she is uncomfortable. I would like to try turning off the overnight feed and simply allowing her to wake when she's hungry so I can nurse her like normal…might try it tonight.

---

[9] From the song: *"Miracles of Miracles"* in *Fiddler on the Roof.*

December 10, 2017, Sunday   1.20

Last night was much better! No more overnight feeds for a while—as long as Colette can keep her weight up.

Tonight will be special because we are taking Colette to church to dedicate her to God. She has always been His, but tonight we will dedicate her life formally to the God Who made her. I'm so excited about it.

December 11, 2017, Monday   1.21

Colette's dedication was so sweet. Just at the last moment when I was looking around waiting to take her up to the platform, I was overwhelmed with such a longing—longing for her to have the chances that I had. I want her to grow up in church, go to youth group, go to camp, and play an instrument in the church orchestra. All I could do was cry out to my Father, asking Him to spare her.

The dedication was beautiful; TJ came up with us and did well right up until the end when he spotted Oma in the crowd. He called out "Oma!" and when Tim picked him up he sneezed <u>right</u> on Colette!

December 12, 2017, Tuesday   1.22

Colette spent her first night sleeping in the crib (as opposed to her swing), and she did really well! TJ, who has been a bit cantankerous since Colette's been home, seems to have banished his evil twin and has returned to his normal, sweet self. He loves "helping" with "Coco" and spends his time fetching things for Mommy and Oma as we work at getting this house back in order.

Outside the snow is falling; inside a pine candle is burning. It is definitely a "God's in His heaven, all's right with the world" kind of day.[10]

December 14, 2017, Thursday   1.24

I believe Colette is going through a growth spurt! She gets so filled with rage then returns to her calm self once she's fed…I've been nursing her plus giving her extra formula through the NG. I'm glad she is so willing to eat because her weight was slightly down at her checkup yesterday [while home, we had a weekly appointment at the outpatient oncology clinic where Dr. Stearns could examine her and blood work

---

[10] From: *"Song from Pippa Passes"* by Robert Browning.

could be obtained]. *Other than that, though, the report was good. Her counts are all rising.*

Dr. Stearns wants us to return to the hospital on Sunday evening to get a head start on round two of chemotherapy. He believes that by coming Sunday night, the first dose of chemotherapy can be given bright and early Monday morning.

December 15, 2017, Friday   1.25

Colette is four months old today! What a darling four month old! She seems to have moved past her growth spurt fussiness and is back to being sweet, calm and beautiful. Meanwhile, I'm running around like a crazy woman trying to get a million things done around here before we have to go back to the hospital.

December 16, 2017, Saturday   1.26

Last night left quite a bit to be desired with regard to sleep! Colette was up nearly every hour to eat. Then TJ, who is usually such good sleeper, decided to join the fun and got up! So...Tim and I are pretty tired today. However, Grammy and Grampy [Tim's parents] *are coming over tonight to see Colette before she starts round two of chemo.*

December 17, 2017, Sunday   1.27

Today is our last day home together, and it is a perfect Christmassy Day. We have snow on the ground and coziness inside. TJ and Colette continue their poor sleep routine (TJ got up twice!) much to Tim's and my chagrin.

However, Christmas is coming, whether we have energy for it or not! So in the holiday spirit, TJ, Tim and I made sugar cookies for Santa (I put them in the freezer for Tim and TJ to set out Christmas Eve). TJ <u>loved</u> the sprinkles—who doesn't?

CHAPTER 6

The Second Round

D*ecember 18, 2017, Monday*   *2.1*
What a "terrible, horrible, no good, very bad day."[11] We survived, but wow, the meltdowns!

    Last night was difficult enough having to leave TJ…to hear him say "Bye Coco, Bye Momma!" as cheerily as if he was simply leaving to go to the park instead of leaving with Oma to be separated from Colette for the next three weeks. I cried and cried as Tim, Colette and I left for the hospital. Kayla met us on our arrival to help us unpack and set up our new room. Kayla is like my good fairy—when she appears things get better, my smile gets bigger, my heart feels lighter. I am so thankful for such a wonderful sister. With her help our small, oddly shaped triangle room was transformed into a comfortable nest.

    We had a decent night until 6:00 AM when it was time to put in Colette's Foley catheter. What a nightmare. The nurses tried multiple times to put the Foley in, and finally after many tears (both from Colette and me who had the miserable job of attempting to hold her still), they got a doctor from the NICU to come place it.

    Next, the nurses had to place a new NG. This too was a traumatizing ordeal. After putting it in, the nurses realized that the tube was too long. It was 3 ft long—extending

---

[11] From: *Alexander and the Terrible, Horrible, No Good, Very Bad Day by Judith Viorst.*

from her face like a long leash just waiting to get caught and snagged on anything it came in contact with. Because it was shift change for the nurses and everyone was anxious to escape the screaming cries of an overwrought baby, it was suggested that a new NG be placed by the day shift nurses. Emotionally exhausted at this point, I agreed, and Colette got a bit of reprieve.

Colette was besides herself during the second attempt to place the NG. However, it was eventually in place, and she was tucked into her swing where she drifted into a most well-deserved nap. The room was finally quiet for a couple of minutes. But less than ten minutes into her sleep, Colette was woken by two nurses who entered the room to start her chemo. She became completely inconsolable...high-pitched crying and back arching. I tried everything to calm her down and finally got her settled by laying her flat on her back in the crib while I patted her sides. We were told that she was having bladder spasms from all the trauma that occurred during the Foley placement attempts. She was put on Tylenol and Ditropan and has since calmed down. The doctors discussed taking the Foley out, but I'm glad to say it is still in and is doing fine.

We were later moved to a double room which is similar to our last one and gives us more space. The ending of our day has been much calmer than the beginning. Colette is getting continuous feeds tonight as she ate poorly all day...no surprise there!

December 19, 2017, Tuesday   *2.2*

Last night was a success! Colette slept beautifully and had no issues with her all-night feeds. We slept well too!

Her fussiness has subsided so she no longer needs Tylenol. She has had a chest x-ray and an EKG done, which is standard protocol in preparation for the stem cell collection that is scheduled for the end of this round of chemotherapy.

I will be going home soon to be with Tim and TJ tonight while Mom and Dad stay with Colette. I can't wait to see my little guy!

December 20, 2017, Wednesday   *2.3*

Colette continues to do well—no nausea and vomiting. She did have a little blood in her urine before I left yesterday, but even that has cleared up (they believe it was from the trauma of the Foley insertion).

Dr. Dallas (who is her stem cell transplant doctor) is the attending doctor for the week which has allowed us to learn more about the upcoming stem cell collection and eventual transplants.

On the home front, TJ is sweet and wonderful! He is obsessed with the Christmas lights—love being here with him.

December 21, 2017, Thursday   *2.4*

Happy Anniversary to Tim and I! Five years ago today, we were in the last minute bustle before the ceremony. Kayla, Mom, and I were hiding in one of the tiny Sunday school classrooms waiting for the "all-clear" to come out! That day was one of the most beautiful days of my life—so much snow, gold, red and sparkle! Followed by a week in Colonial Williamsburg…glorious!

Back to reality, Colette is getting her Foley out today. Hopefully that will relieve any pain she is having. Mom said she was awake and crying hard around midnight and needed Tylenol and Ditropan. She had more "trace" amounts of blood in her urine, but the doctors are attributing that to the Foley. The Cisplatin [one of the chemotherapy drugs] *she got yesterday seems to be the one that gives her the most trouble, but she still hasn't vomited.*

Meanwhile I've been home with TJ. We played like mad-men in the basement with the Christmas lights adding festive joy. Later we painted pictures and wrestled. He loves rough-housing—as do I, no complaints here!

Tonight, Kayla will get TJ while Tim and I go to dinner and then to Severance Hall [the performance hall for the Cleveland Orchestra located just opposite of the hospital] *for their Christmas performance. I'm extremely excited—afterwards we will spend the night with Colette.*

December 22, 2017, Friday   *2.5*

What a strange day! But to go in order, I'll start with last night…Tim and I had an amazing night at Severance Hall. The orchestra was overpowering—I wanted to dance and cry and sing but settled for tapping my foot with enthusiasm! Our dinner, however, was not such a success. We went to Little Italy but couldn't find anywhere to park. Once we did finally manage to squeeze ourselves into a spot, we couldn't get a table anywhere.

When we finally got a table, we couldn't get a meal! After waiting about an hour we had to leave for fear of being too late to the performance! We thought we could just get dessert at Prestis, but the line was out the door…perhaps Panera on the way? Couldn't find it! Running out of time, Tim parked the car, and we hustled on foot to Severance Hall while eating a piece of pizza from a random pizza shop we found en route. Tim got a bag of chips and a cookie at the concession table at Severance Hall and that was our meal to remember! But the music soon helped us forget our woes…

After the performance, we walked back to the hospital. My mom had just gotten Colette back to sleep following an episode of vomiting. Colette was given Ativan to combat the nausea (it's now been scheduled around the clock in order to keep ahead of the nausea and vomiting), and the nurses slowed down her NG feeds so that her stomach has more time to digest them.

This morning I was shocked to see how swollen her face was. She was also very pale which makes sense as I learned in rounds that her red blood cell count was low. She was scheduled to have a blood transfusion. Meanwhile, she was calm, content and sleepy. Tim returned in the afternoon (he had to go to work in the morning), and while she was getting her blood transfusion, I told the nurse that she just didn't look right. She was so swollen, pale and lethargic. The nurse got the resident doctor and the fellow who put her on a cardiac monitor. Her heart rate was in the 180s; respirations were upper 40s, and blood pressures were 70s over 40s. She also wasn't tracking with her eyes very well. In came more nurses and eventually the attending doctor. Before long a PACT was called [PACTs could be called by health care workers or family who were concerned that a patient was declining; once called, a PICU doctor and nurse would come to evaluate the patient, provide care and determine whether a transfer to the PICU was needed].

Colette perked up after the arrival of the PICU fellow and nurse (which happened to be one of our favorites, Jenn!). Her blood pressure rose, and heart rate went back down. Puzzled as to what had happened, the doctor requested that the neurology team assess her to rule out a seizure. She also ordered a CT scan.

Hours went by with many eyes on Colette; and although she was fussy, she did seem to return to her normal self. She finished her blood transfusion and got her CT scan which showed no brain bleed, hydrocephalus or (the best part) any sign of tumor regrowth!

She's sleeping now, and I hope to follow suit.

In the midst of this, we were visited by "Jeremy Cares" an organization started by a family who stayed here over Christmas in 2008 while one of their sons was undergoing treatment for cancer and the other son was recovering from surgery (he had one of his kidneys removed to donate to his brother!). They came with giant bags of gifts for our whole family…one of which is a motorized mini four wheeler! I can't wait to give it to TJ!

Amazing, exhausting, relieving day.

Goodnight!

December 23, 2017, Saturday   *2.6*

   This morning at 6:00 AM Colette had a fever. They drew cultures (so far all negative) and started her on antibiotics. Her vital signs have all been normal, and she has better color. They are suspicious of a UTI (although not overwhelmingly convinced) so urine cultures were taken as well. Thankfully, she has not had any fevers since this morning; hopefully this will amount to nothing. She's been started on Tylenol and oxycodone for pain which has helped with her fussiness. All in all, she is not herself—in a sad but not scary way.

December 27, 2017, Wednesday   *2.10*

   Christmas and my birthday have come and gone, and we are all doing well! Christmas Eve went smoothly—Kayla and I decorated the room with everything we got from Jeremy Cares (a little tree and colored lights, etc.), and we set up all the presents. There were more presents than I've ever seen for two little people. It was so festive and jolly in the room.

   Colette seemed more herself with the pain medicine. She slept, woke, cooed and slept some more. Mom and Dad came in the afternoon while I went home. Tim and I enjoyed TJ to the fullest! We "romped" on the bed which involves TJ "pushing" us off the bed with all his might while saying "Go Dada/Go Momma!" then peeking his head over the side of the bed to inquire "Are you okay?" and repeat.

   TJ was eventually tucked into bed after we read the Christmas story from Luke 2 and set out cookies for Santa. Tim and I then filled TJ and Colette's stockings, and I set off for the hospital with Kayla who intended to spend Christmas Eve with us.

   We found Colette still up with Poppa and Oma and full of Christmas cheer. We decorated her crib with a Baby's First Christmas blanket and a new Peter Rabbit Christmas book. We then set up an extra cot in the side room where we ate fudge and fruit salad! Before putting Colette down for the night, we read her "The Night before Christmas" using Poppa's childhood book. After a prayer, I laid her down to sleep. Such sweet moments can't really be described, they must simply be remembered and cherished. She slept well (only one vomiting episode at 6 AM) as did Dad, Mom and I in our cots in the adjacent room.

In the morning, Tim and TJ came filling the room with joy! TJ (although excited about the presents) was more interested in finding Coco! My parents went for a walk around Wade Pond while Tim and I began opening presents with TJ. Colette contentedly watched the festive ordeal from her perch in her little swing. So many delights for TJ—the climax of which being the mini four wheeler which we hid for him in the shower! He was absolutely delighted with it until he discovered that the fearsome thing <u>moved</u>. Not only did it move on its own, but it made a terrible, loud noise! After that, it was "No! No!" to his new possession. He even put his foot down in protest, refusing to let his stuffed rabbit Flossie ride it! He will apparently need to warm up to this great and mighty vehicle.

Kayla and my parents joined us at this point, and we finished opening gifts. Tim and TJ stayed for an incredible steak dinner brought to us by the kindest people from A Special Wish Foundation. After lunch, Tim and TJ went to Grammy and Grampy's for the rest of the day.

At the hospital, we feasted, played games, laughed and enjoyed Colette's first Christmas to the fullest. We took turns braving the cold (it was in the teens and ever so windy!) and walking around Wade Pond…my pond! It was a worthy sacrifice to see such beauty. The snow, the frozen pond, the geese—breath-taking! Just a perfect Christmas day. In the evening, my mom and I took a final walk to drink in the evening glory. I left to go home around eight in the evening and was able to tuck TJ into bed when he got home from his grandparents, heavy laden with treasures and joy.

The next morning (my birthday!), Tim, TJ and I spent the early hours together until TJ had to go down for a nap. I then drove to the hospital where I found Mom, Kayla, McLaine and Colette. The room was adorned and bedecked with pink and happiness. Well, Colette was adorned with pink, and the rest of the crew was bedecked with happiness! We enjoyed the day with Colette who continued to do well. The stem cell collection team came to the room to discuss the upcoming procedure. They are scheduling it for next week.[12]

---

[12] As I mentioned earlier, the stem cell collection was necessary due to the potency of the chemotherapy medications that were to be used during Colette's last three rounds of chemotherapy. The drugs had such a powerful ability to destroy the rapidly growing tumor cells that they would inadvertently destroy Colette's bone marrow. Without bone marrow, she was susceptible to infections that could potentially be fatal. This created the need for "rescue" stem cell transplants. Stem cells were to be collected from Colette prior to the use of the potent chemotherapy medications through a stem cell harvest. Blood would be drawn out of a large apheresis catheter and run through a machine that would separate the blood,

Today however, they had planned on doing an MRI to see 1. if there were any signs of tumor regrowth and 2. if her brain stem had shifted upwards to a safe location to allow for a lumbar puncture (which will check for tumor cells in her cerebral spinal fluid.) [Her brain stem, which is the lowest part of the brain, had moved down because of pressure from the initial tumor and had remained in an area that made it dangerous to perform lumbar punctures. A lumbar puncture involves the insertion of a needle into the area around the spinal cord to remove a sample of cerebrospinal fluid. This sample could then be examined for tumor cells. If tumor cells were found, it would mean that the tumor was spreading to different areas in the brain and spinal cord.]

I went with Colette to the sedation unit where she was scheduled to be sedated for the MRI, but the Propofol [a sedating medication that was intended to make Colette sleepy enough to hold still for the hour long MRI] *merely dropped her blood pressure and relaxed her airways causing her oxygen levels to drop without making her the least bit still! After three unsuccessful hours in the sedation unit, I returned with Colette to the room. The new plan is for an MRI plus an hearing test under general anesthesia on Friday. We will see.*

Last bit of big news: I made Colette laugh! My first time getting a chuckle out of her!

December 28, 2017, Thursday   *2.11*

Colette had another good night (she only vomited once at 5:30 AM). However, last night was one of the rare nights that I was here alone with her. Usually I have one other person with me to share in the troubles and add some joy. But last night it was just Colette and I. On nights when I am alone, there is a strange sweetness, an increased sense of the presence of God. I truly am not alone—my Father is here with me. Not only is He here with me; He is sad with me. He enters into my sorrow and shares it. I read Psalms 16 before going to bed and echoed David's words, "Because He is at my right hand" because He is here with me—my heart is glad, my glory rejoices, I rest in hope. God will not leave my soul in this hell, and in His presence there is fullness of joy.

First thing at eight this morning two (male) nurses came in for the change of shift report while I was nursing Colette and told me that Colette was scheduled to have her MRI today instead of tomorrow...so stop nursing her please! (A message probably as awkward

---

isolating and storing stem cells. Colette was required to be under heavy sedation in the PICU during this procedure. The entire process would take one to two days depending on how quickly the stem cells could be collected. The stem cells would then be stored and given back to Colette on specific "transplant days" during her last three rounds of chemotherapy.

to give as to receive!) By 11:30 I had her ready to go, and we made our way down to the PACU [Post-Anesthesia Care Unit; a unit devoted to caring for patients immediately before and immediately after being placed under general anesthesia] *where she was to be put under general anesthesia for the MRI. I held her in my arms while she slept, and around noon the anesthesiologist was ready for her. The staff here at Rainbow really is incredible. The amount of people I admire and love grows daily! There is so much skill, knowledge, and above all kindness among them that a mom can't help but make heroes out of so many! However, there are a <u>few</u> exceptions. The anesthesia resident that was on today happened to be one of them. How difficult it is to put Colette into the hands of a stranger; how much greater the difficulty is when the stranger appears to be completely indifferent to the child I am handing over to him! Apathy seemed to be written across his face, and yet I had to entrust my most precious treasure to him. It was done, however, as there was no other alternative. He walked away with Colette leaving me besides an empty crib in the PACU. Had I not the assurance of Joshua 1:9 that the Lord, her God, was with her; wherever she went, I would have crumbled. But that was not the case nor my response. With tears in my eyes I left to find my mom who was on her way to the hospital, and together we waited for the MRI to be done.*

We got the call around 1:30 PM to come back to the PACU where we found Colette groggy and crying—needing a cuddle.

All is well now—she is napping and getting a transfusion of platelets. We should get the results of the MRI soon.

January 1, 2018, Monday 2.15

Welcome 2018! May you be a year of miracles, a year of joy and a year of God's glory!

I forgot my journal when I went home on Thursday so I have a bit to catch up on, but I can take my time and try to fill in as the day allows…

Thursday night was filled with such peace, joy and RELIEF because the MRI came back showing NOTHING! Praise God—not even one suspicious blip. And yet, there's a strangeness in the joy—I'm happy with the news but not satisfied. It is a "lip-happiness" for I am happy with my lips and my brain but not in my heart. Deep down in my heart there is still such great dread and fear. The news is enough to bring joy to my mind and mouth, for I tell everyone I'm so happy and I think to myself, "This is so wonderful. Thank you, God!" But the results don't budge the dread and fear that is dwelling deep within me.

The news, I hope, will come one day that will finally remove every trace of fear and dread. But not today…not yet.

Still, I am thankful. Enough rambling! The MRI revealed that the brain stem is still too far down for a safe lumbar puncture, so that will still have to wait. For now, Dr. Stearns is pleased with the results and plans another full brain and spine MRI in two months.

I went home on Friday and spent the day with Tim and TJ. We all went to his parents to see Mike, Jenna and the girls [Tim's brother and family who were in town visiting from Florida]. *It was so nice to see everyone! TJ enjoyed himself immensely with his cousins as evidenced by his exhaustion. He took nice long naps and went to bed without a single complaint every day I was home.*

On Sunday, Tim, TJ, and I went to church; then after putting TJ down for a nap at my parents (with Kayla there to watch him), Tim and I scooted off to the hospital.

How was Colette these days? Per the reports from my parents, very well at first. She got a blood transfusion on Friday without any complications and a platelet transfusion on Saturday. Her ANC started coming up, which is perfect timing for the planned stem cell collection [the stem cell collection works best if it is done just as the ANC begins its rapid upward climb. The problem is that *when* this will happen is really a matter of guesswork on the part of the doctors!]

Saturday night, however, Colette got increasingly irritable and began vomiting. She was started on oxycodone and Benadryl but still was struggling. Poor Mom had a difficult time as apparently all Colette wanted was to be held by my mom ALONE. Every attempt to transfer her to my dad or her crib left Colette enraged! When Tim and I took over on Sunday, Colette was irritable but not inconsolable. I made a couple changes which I hope will help 1. breast milk only through the NG (to see if she tolerates it better than the breast milk fortified with formula) 2. Oxycodone around the clock as they believe she is having bone pain which I am told is common when the ANC is rising. [We learned to dread this "bone pain" in subsequent rounds. Colette always struggled horribly with it even though it was a sign that everything was moving in the right direction. We were told by older patients that the bone pain associated with the rising ANC felt like the joint and muscle aches of the flu which made any movement unpleasant.]. *So far she seems a little better.*

She slept beautifully from 10:00 PM-9:00 AM (besides her normal 5:00 AM diaper change, vital sign check, blood drawing, medication administration and Neupogen shot [a shot that was given to her daily which stimulated her bone marrow to help raise the ANC faster but which also caused the notorious bone pain]*). She has been content on the new pain management regimen, and we were even able to do physical therapy with her.*

She is scheduled to have surgery tomorrow at 7:30 AM for the placement of her apheresis catheter [A line, similar to an IV but much larger, that would go through one of the veins in her neck. It would be used to remove blood for the stem cell collection]. *She will get platelets today to prepare her for the surgery. Her ANC is up to 0.3 (it was 0.03 yesterday). All will continue as planned for the stem cell collection on Wednesday.*

As for my hopes for this new year, I am hoping for a miracle. I am hoping that Colette will be healed, cancer free without any long-term complications. I am hoping that I see God more accurately—that I will know Him more and love Him more. I am hoping that my mind is filled with truth and that I think more biblically and act more biblically daily. I am hoping to have a stronger marriage and to love Tim more. I am hoping to be a stronger, more competent mom. I hope I bring God more glory this year than I have ever before.

January 2, 2018, Tuesday   *2.16*

    Colette had her apheresis catheter placed this morning. Though I was up at 5:30 AM, I left waking Colette till the last possible minute. When it was time, I gently woke her, changed her, took her vitals and gave her the Neupogen shot before setting off with the nurse to the PACU. It was much nicer this time because the anesthesia team was made up of young mom-type women who made me feel much more at ease handing her over.

    Colette truly was amazing. It made me cry to watch her. I handed her to the anesthesiologist, and she looked right up into the stranger's face. Her eyes filled with fear and sadness...fear from being in a stranger's arms and sadness because she had been so cozy and now she was not. Still, she did not cry. She has never cried when going to a surgery...I have, however, nearly every time. The pain of handing your baby to a stranger and watching them walk away—aghhh! It is such a terrible, terrible ache. Tim left to go home and prepare the house for her (hopeful) discharge soon. I came back to the room to get things organized (including myself) and to pray.

I was soon called back to the PACU waiting room, and the doctor told me she was doing well but still recovering. It was about a half hour before I could go see her; and after going over some verses and praying, I foolishly looked online. Colette has been having difficulty nursing, or more accurately, has not been wanting to nurse *at all*. I wanted to see if I could find something on breastfeeding a baby during chemotherapy…I found two articles. Nothing else. It then struck me how rare our situation is—how alone I am in this experience. Both articles were written by the moms themselves and neither were moms of babies as young as Colette. Both of the children had months of experience breastfeeding before starting chemotherapy, unlike Colette who had only a couple of weeks to learn her skill. It was like I was Peter in the Bible—I had been calmly walking on water, and suddenly I looked around at the others and what was normal. I began to sink [Matt. 14: 25-33]. The thought came, "What am I doing? What is going on?—This is not normal!" But I will fix my eyes back on my God. I will keep walking on water. There is no need for doubting; He will guide.

PS: In the waiting room of the PACU there is a giant picture of the earth from the view of space. I love it because every time Colette has a surgery, I look up at it and am reminded that she is in the hands of my Father…and what are His credentials? Oh, just "the maker of heaven and earth." [Psalm 121:1-2]

January 3, 2018, Wednesday   2.17

My mom and I got up (after a most unrestful night of sleep filled with too many thoughts) at 5:30 AM to get ready for Colette's transfer to the PICU for the stem cell harvest. We left the oncology floor around 6:00 AM. It is so strange being back in the PICU. I love the fast-paced, eager, competent nurses and doctors. I just feel <u>SAFE</u>! The oncology floor is wonderful, but when it comes to security, there is nothing like the PICU with its mass of brilliant minds ever ready for a challenge. And I'm glad, because we brought a few challenges with us.

First of all, Colette needed an additional IV before starting the procedure. At first just a peripheral line was discussed, but the apheresis team then made the decision that both an arterial and a peripheral line would be needed. To accomplish this, two PICU attending doctors sedated Colette while Mom and I kept our old vigil in the "Serenity Room." We have shared many a tear and many a laugh in that room. We've prayed, made phone calls and (only me!) have pumped in that room! After half an hour, one of the doctors told us that the arterial line was in, but Colette had not done well with the Propofol they had used for sedation. Just as before, the medication caused her blood pressure and oxygen levels to drop while she continued to wiggle about. Because of this, they decided it would not be safe to attempt to sedate her with Propofol for the stem cell collection. Instead, they would need to do heavy sedation and put her on a ventilator. She left us to digest this information while the peripheral line was placed.

We were allowed to see Colette again before her intubation, and she was so sweet and beautiful—all wiggly and goofy from the Propofol. She just smiled at my mom and me with a glazed look in spite of the tubes and IVs that were coming out all over her. *What an amazing girl!*

We waited again in the Serenity Room while she was intubated. There was some difficulty about getting it in the right spot, but all was soon resolved and the collection was started around noon. It is now 2:30 PM, and the team has about an hour left of collection. Colette is doing well. When they finish, it will take about two hours to analyze what has been collected. The goal is to obtain 90 million stem cells. If they have enough, they will extubate and remove the apheresis catheter. If not, she will remain in the PICU on the ventilator overnight for more collection tomorrow.

If it does come out—we will go back to the oncology floor and potentially be discharged on Thursday or Friday!

7:30 PM

They got 101,400,000! No need for collection tomorrow! God is so good! She will be extubated soon, then remain in the PICU all night for monitoring. Her apheresis catheter comes out tomorrow…then plans for home! Also, the results of her hearing test (which they did while she was sedated) are back showing no hearing loss!

January 5, 2018, Friday   2.19

We are home! Yesterday was a long day of waiting at the hospital. We waited for the arterial line to come out. We waited for the peripheral line to come out. We waited for the apheresis catheter to come out. We waited for a transfer back to the oncology floor; and finally, we waited for a discharge home! Colette was a wee bit more fussy than normal, most likely due to all her poor body has gone through the past couple of days. By 8:00 in the evening, we were home.

Before we arrived TJ had been shipped off to my parents because he had a cold and we were afraid to let him near Colette. Tim and I got Colette settled as quickly as we could, but it wasn't as smooth as we would have liked because we forgot all our frozen breastmilk at the hospital and the discharge instructions were missing Colette's Keppra dosing [seizure medicine]! I made several phone calls to get the information we needed while Tim ran back up to the hospital to pick up the missing milk.

Colette then had a ghastly night (as did Tim and I by default). She was up nearly every hour and multiple times in between. It was a discouraging start to our time home, and as her fussiness has continued today, my joy at being home is somewhat subdued. Plus, I see piles of laundry and three weeks of disorganization to undo…added to the fact that Colette isn't nursing very well! Meanwhile my phone is exploding with texts of congratulations for us being home. I am thankful to be home. I am thankful Colette is home, but it is exhausting being here.

January 8, 2017, Monday   2.22

I can't believe how busy we are! On Saturday, TJ came home for a while but didn't stay long because his cold had gotten worse. Tim whisked him off to Grammy and Grampy's while I stayed home with Colette and just cried. My little family! McLaine came before long to salvage the situation from utter despair!

Colette had another difficult night and was up every hour. She vomited around six in the morning and a couple more times throughout the day.

On Sunday Tim returned while TJ went to my parent's house. I have such an ache for TJ. It hurts so badly to know he is living his life, and I am not a permanent fixture in it. He doesn't wake up knowing that whatever else changes or will happen that day, he can count on "mommy" being there. It pains me—but a lot in my life pains me. If I didn't know that God is sovereign, I would be crushed and petrified. But God is *sovereign, so I know I can trust that this* too *will be for good.*

My life is so messy right now—all the order, consistency, and safety is gone. God has uprooted every fixture in my life but Himself. Those I love are present then vanish. My home is not my own little kingdom of joy but a mere place to sleep. My time is uncertain— I do not know what to expect from one hour to the next let alone from one day to the next. Everything I have loved in my life has been torn up and scattered. It is only God Whom I see and know as familiar. He is the same God who has comforted me since I was a child. I know *Him, and He is the same. I love Him, and oh, Father, I want to please You. Help me bring You glory in spite of my weakness.*

January 10, 2018, Wednesday   2.24

Total meltdown today—all the big things are fine, but every itty-bitty little thing is an absolute mess.

TJ came home last night and has been as clingy as a leech and as touchy as a beauty queen losing her looks. As for Colette, she has taken to arching and crying for hours on end with no apparent reason. She is starting again, so I will close.

Later

My mom came to help with the littles which truly has been life-saving. I can honestly say it was utter chaos until she came through the door. I got up this morning to pump before either were up only to hear TJ calling for me midway through pumping. This woke up Colette, who (because she was still tired) screamed and cried without stopping until I managed to get her to sleep an hour-and-a-half later. I just went back and forth between TJ and Colette. They were in an all-out competition to see who could cry louder. They both won! TJ cried because he wanted me to sit and hold him; Colette cried because she wanted me to walk and hold her. It was a loud morning. Even when mom came, it was a hectic mad dash of trying, not to keep one step ahead, but merely keep up with the two.

Tim came home in the afternoon to join me as I took Colette to her clinic visit which involved PT, OT, a lactation consultation, and a visit with Dr. Stearns. PT thinks she is doing well but gave us a few stretches and exercises to try. OT gave us some new tips to help Colette with the bottle, and lactation gave me some help with the breast-feeding issues. She did drop a little in her weight (probably from all the vomiting episodes). They made plans to increase her calories by fortifying the breast milk with formula again. Dr. Stearns is all-around pleased with her. The next round will start on Monday. We will take her to the outpatient clinic in the morning to have her labs drawn; then she will get admitted. She will also need another hearing screen, a kidney function test and a second Broviac placed this round.

Hope to be home at the beginning of February after round three of chemotherapy. After today, the thought of being home is not as sweet as it has been in the past. Our nights have been splattered with tears, meltdowns and not-so-kind words. Not ideal.

January 11, 2018, Thursday   2.25

Today went much better as Tim stayed home in the morning until my mom arrived. TJ continues to be quite a challenge. He had a melt down in the parking lot at the grocery store which wasn't very pleasant. I took him to get us both out of the house as it has been warm today (upper 50s!).

My mom helped me get things in better order around the house. Still, it has really been challenging, straining, and just plain hard this time at home!

On the positive side, Colette is breastfeeding a little better.

January 13, 2018, Saturday   *2.27*

Happy Birthday to Poppa! He got the biggest blizzard of the year for his birthday (which just so happens to be his heart's desire!)

On the home front, things continue to be difficult, but at least now we seem to have an answer as to Colette's difficulties—she has a cold!

Last night I gave a remarkable demonstration of total depravity as I tried to manage every emotion from confusion to frustration to fear and sadness. I did not manage them well. Colette was crying inconsolably hour after hour while TJ bounced between being a ray of sunshine and a cloud of despair. Grammy and Grampy came for a visit, but as the roads were getting worse and the littles were out of sorts, they left shortly after their arrival. That night Colette began getting congested and developed a little cough. She slept horribly. Tim and I took turns holding her. It was a long night, but not as difficult as the night before because I was filled with sympathy for a sick baby, not filled with frustration with a baby who was refusing to sleep—there is a huge difference. Ask any mother.

We talked with the doctor on-call because this was her first sickness while she has been home. We were told to watch for fevers (she had none). She has slept for hours in my arms today and appears much more comfortable.

January 15, 2018, Monday   *2.28*

Mom and Dad picked up TJ last night around six, giving Tim and I time to pack and prepare for the start of round three of chemotherapy. It is always hard breaking up the family. It's hard giving kisses and telling TJ to say goodbye to "Coco." Hard to watch him give her a kiss on the head out of obligation then seeing him look back at her and return to give her a couple pats on the belly out of pure love. They are so sweet together. It hurts to pull them apart.

On Sunday Tim had taken TJ to Build-a-Bear for an event put on by A Special Wish. TJ was tasked with the responsibility of making something for Colette. He said "no" to every animal he saw until he spotted a rainbow unicorn! He stuffed it and brought it home for Colette, along with a stuffed car he got for himself into which he manages to squeeze himself and Flossie! Colette enjoyed looking at her colorful new unicorn but had more fun watching TJ scamper in circles around her. He talks incessantly as he jumps and plays in her room—occasionally stopping to give her some pats on the head or belly while saying *"Oh…Coco"* which produces the biggest grin on her face. Once during his play, I saw him stop. He must have noticed that her socks had fallen off because before I knew it he was kneeling in front of her trying to put her pink sock back on her wiggly little foot!

This morning, Tim and I took Colette to the outpatient clinic where her labs were to be drawn to make sure her ANC was high enough to start chemo (they wanted it above 1.0). It came back at 0.84. Dr. Stearns believes it may be down slightly from her cold (it had been 1.05 on Wednesday). He decided to postpone the start of chemo until Thursday (if her counts are back up by then). So here we are back at home!

I *was* nervous and felt sick about the delay in treatment, but I keep turning my mind to truth. My faith is in a living, all-wise, all-powerful God Who created all things and knows no limitations. My faith is *not* in following a protocol. So I *can* rest in peace.

It's snowing outside…I'm sitting in my little kitchen listening to Colette's soft breathing as she sleeps in her car seat, having fallen asleep on the way home from the clinic.

I started this journal on the day of Colette's birth. I started it by saying she has transformed my world, and now that I've reached the end of this journal, I will close it by echoing those same words. She *has* transformed my world. But what is greater is that God is using her to transform me. She truly is a good and perfect gift.

Thank you God for these five months with her—You have been so good!

[New Journal]
January 16, 2018, Tuesday   2.29

This is her story…the story of my strong, sweet daughter Colette. But this is also *our* story—the story of the Piazza family and the army of warriors surrounding us. The pages of this new journal will contain the great victories as well as the stinging defeats of the months ahead. In the end, this will be *His* story—the story our good Father writes for us, may we all walk worthy.

January 17, 2018, Wednesday   2.30

We have had a cozy day here at Meadowbrook. Both of the littles slept well, which means that Tim and I both slept well. Just a couple pacifier runs and one pumping session! Colette woke before TJ, which was nice because I was able to get her going for the day (diaper changed, nursed, medications given, and NG feeds set up) before getting TJ up and going. Things went beautifully all morning.

Colette still has the sniffles but is much improved. Tomorrow we take her back to see if her ANC is high enough to start chemotherapy. My mom will take TJ home with her later tonight…sad night ahead.

CHAPTER 7

The Third Round

January 19, Friday   3.2

We have begun round three! Yesterday we took Colette to the outpatient clinic at 10:00 in the morning where she got her RSV vaccine and had her labs drawn. Her ANC was over 1.7! God certainly answered that prayer! Her weight had also increased which was good news.

We got our room on the oncology floor around two o'clock that afternoon. It is a small single room. If I were not reading a missionary story about women raising their children in unbelievable circumstances, I would have despaired! But I am, so I did not! We are as cozy as possible in the room. We had two PICU nurses come to place her Foley catheter, which made it a much smoother process than the last insertion. She did cry for about a half-hour afterwards but calmed down with Tylenol and snuggles.

Her first dose of chemo was given last night; and although she had a difficult beginning to her night, she slept soundly after 1:00 AM. She has been sleepy but calm today. My parents will stay with her tonight.

January 20, 2018, Saturday   3.3

My mom gave us a good report on Colette (no vomiting and no nausea medications needed). She continues to be sleepy and content.

TJ and I spent the morning together as Tim met with a friend for breakfast. Later, TJ and Tim went sledding which, by all accounts, was wonderful!

January 21, 2018, Sunday   *3.4*

I'm back at the hospital, but what a lovely morning with TJ. I feel like a kid slowly trying to get every last drop out of a freeze pop—I'm trying to savor every moment with TJ. At one point in the morning, we were laying on the bed, and I was singing to him "You are my Sunshine" while he lay beside me with a dazed look, twirling his hair into a curly knot. He sat up after a bit to go grab his blanket in the other room; I stopped singing. The moment I stopped he turned back around and said, "Sunshine? Sunshine?" so back to the song I went until he returned with the desired blanket. Could I love him more? I don't think so!

Church was beautiful as usual, and afterwards we took TJ to my parents where I fed him and put him down for his nap. Kayla and Dad stayed with him while Tim and I returned to the hospital.

Miss Colette's day has circled around her need for a blood transfusion. Her red blood cell count was low this morning. I found this out at church, and through a texting session back and forth with my mom I was able to give consent to start a transfusion. Since our arrival, Colette has been playful and full of chatter…bliss!

January 22, 2018, Monday   *3.5*

Today felt like a very long day…Colette did well last night (a few pacifier runs and rockings, but nothing terrible). She got up for the day at six am. I tried to convince her to change her mind, but my social girl was not having it! She doesn't seem to have any nausea, and her Foley came out today which is liberating! The only concern I have is her swelling. She has had a 10% weight gain since Thursday (indicating that she's retaining fluid). She got Lasix to increase her urine output, and we will see if that resolves the issue.

January 23, 2018, Tuesday   *3.6*

We have had another good day. Besides one episode of vomiting around six this morning, Colette did well through the night. Her Ativan dose was increased to help with the nausea, and her swelling has gone down (as has her weight) so all is well here! Tim will join us this evening.

January 24, 2018, Wednesday   *3.7*

Colette seems so happy and calm—just what we love to see! We got moved to a double room, and it is the biggest one yet! It was amazing to sleep more soundly. Tim stayed the night with us and slept on Colette's side of the room (like an angel) to do pacifier runs. She did vomit twice today so her Ativan dose will be increased again and her NG feeds will be slowed down. I'll be going home this evening.

January 25, 2018, Thursday   *3.8*

Enjoying a day home with TJ. Sometimes days like these are difficult because they give me a sample, a taste of what <u>could</u> be. I get excited—thinking about the routine, the little world I'd like to create here. I get anxious for these days of separation to be over. I start to long for a "normal" life.

I took TJ to the library, and it just so happened to be during story time. I remember so clearly taking him to it last year. I even saw some familiar faces. When I walked out with TJ I felt discouraged but remembered—this is God's plan for our family. It is different from most families, but I will <u>cheerfully</u> submit. I'm reading <u>Green Leaf in Drought</u> by Isobel Kuhn which is <u>amazing</u>. It is transforming my understanding of trials and making me realize how little I understand what suffering (and suffering well) is.
PS: Colette has had more vomiting episodes. They increased her Ativan. ANC is dropping

January 26, 2018, Friday   *3.9*

I'm back at the hospital with Miss Colette. She hasn't vomited since yesterday. Her feeds have been slowed down which has helped her tolerate them. However, she has been more fussy than normal and has been started on Tylenol and oxycodone (which has helped).

She received a platelet transfusion today and is supposed to get a transfusion of IgG [a blood product that contains the antibody IgG which is needed for the body to fight infections]. McLaine and Mom joined me today, and as it is a sunny day, I took the opportunity to walk around Wade Pond—oh, how glorious the sun is!
PS: ANC is 0.01 and dropping

January 27, 2018, Saturday   *3.10*

Colette's ANC was 0 this morning, and she had a fever at 5:00 AM. She was put on antibiotics and (thankfully) has not had a fever since. I've been home today while my mom is with Colette. She says that Colette has been sleepy all day and that the Tylenol and oxycodone has kept her pain under control.

Meanwhile, Tim and I took TJ to a basketball game at Tim's school and to the zoo as it was nearly 50 degrees outside. TJ loved it all! It was so nice being able to run and play with him. It is only when I see other young families and hear them talking and making plans that my spirit sinks. That <u>was</u> me. That <u>was</u> us!

January 29, 2018, Monday   *3.12*

Back in room 6026! Colette is doing well although her ANC still hasn't come up (it was 0.02 yesterday and back to 0 again today). She hasn't had any more fevers and has been more herself, which is wonderful. She did vomit once last evening. Other than that, the only news is that her platelets are low. She had a bloody nose and petechiae [a small red rash that appears on the skin when platelets are low] *on her legs this morning. She is scheduled to get a platelet transfusion later today.*

An MRI of her brain and spine, as well as a hearing screen, will be done on Wednesday around 1:00 PM. They also mentioned that they may need to do an eye exam and a CT scan of her abdomen to establish baselines before her stem cell transplant…we will learn about that in more detail soon, I'm sure.

I remember these days at the hospital so vividly. It seemed our world had shrunk so small. There was one main character and a few supporting actors. This little circle absorbed all our time and all our thoughts. As these journal entries portray, our minds revolved around medical check lists. We would dream and hope in terms of ANC levels, NG feed rates and vital sign changes. Exams and procedures were the hurdles set between us and our craving for ultimate victory. After conquering one, we would fix our eyes on the next…and the next…This had become our world, and my writings at the time give evidence to this fact. And yet, in the midst of this race there was never a loss of focus. We were battling to secure Colette's life, but our longing to cherish her for years did not make us forget that we currently had been given these moments. Colette was cherished. She was feasted on by us all with an insatiable appetite. We made her laugh; we sung her songs, we read her books; we held her close. The lab work, the vital signs, the test results merely tell the subplot. The real story was the never ending quest to envelop her in love.

January 30, 2018, Tuesday   *3.13*

Colette had a difficult evening last night. She got an early dose of oxycodone plus some Tylenol which helped eventually; she slept soundly after 1:30 AM.

Today she's been doing very well, only fussing before naps. The big news is that she drank a whole ounce of milk out of her new pink sippy cup! This is the first time ever! She hasn't been nursing well, so maybe this will help.

Tomorrow is the big day—she has her MRI and hearing screening plus possibly her kidney and vision exam. Later in the week she will get a CT of the abdomen and pelvis in preparation for her stem cell transplant. Her ANC is still 0. I've begun thinking about how to start her on solids and how to help her sleep better when we get home! I'm praying for wisdom on how to move forward. Strangely, there are no Pinterest articles on sleep-training your baby during chemo, but I do have the resource of an all-wise Father.

January 31, 2018, Wednesday   3.14

They just took her for the MRI and hearing screen.

February 1, 2018, Thursday   3.15

Picking up from yesterday, my mom came in the late afternoon while I was waiting for the completion of Colette's MRI. The whole process took about three to four hours. She was, once again, as brave as a lion when she went back for anesthesia—and oh, so snuggly! The team of anesthesiologists were all caring people, which made the "hand-off" easier.

The first results were from the audiologist—no change to her hearing! Dr. Stearns came to our room around 5:00 that evening to give us the MRI results…NO TUMOR! The scans showed nothing even suspicious. He said this is very encouraging because some tumors would have already returned by this point. Praise God—what a glorious gift! He told us that the brain stem is still too low for a lumbar puncture. However, he commented on the fact that she has had no hearing loss by saying it was "remarkable." He had expected some hearing changes by now. The next MRI will be done at the end of the next three rounds of chemotherapy at which point it may be safe to do a lumbar puncture. Based on those results, the next steps will be determined: radiation, no radiation, more chemo…we will see.

PS: ANC is 0; platelet transfusion today

February 2, 2018, Friday   3.16

Colette continues to do well even though her ANC continues to be sluggish. It was 0.01 today. Apparently, we will not be going home this weekend. Meanwhile, she continues to give us hope about sleeping better. She has been sleeping from 8:30 PM-6:00 AM without waking at all (I only get up to pump and let the nurses know when machines are beeping etc.) I keep praying for wisdom on how to help her establish good sleep habits with all she's going through. She nursed a little twice today and took a little from her sippy cup. Her feeds have also been increased.

More exciting news: she got the all-clear to start solids! We found a high chair and bib...just waiting for the rice cereal. I hope to attempt it at her 6:00 evening feed.
PS: She's starting to get more fussy...maybe the bone pain is kicking into high gear, and we will see some increased counts soon!

February 3, 2018, Saturday   *3.17*
Colette's counts are still near zero, and she needs blood today. My mom said she was up nearly every hour last night but has been happy and content today.

As for the attempt at solid food, it was a success! I gave her the rice cereal before leaving last evening. The staff was so excited—everyone buzzing around to gather supplies (bib, high chair, spoons and the cereal, of course). She did super! She kept kicking her little feet with joy. She ate more than anyone expected—way to go Colette!

At home with the boys today. TJ's been a crafter...playing with play dough and painting.

February 4, 2018, Sunday   *3.18*
Back at the hospital. It is hard to come, and it is hard to go. Each child seems to twist their little soul roots into my heart. Every time I leave one of them, I have to tear up those roots, and it hurts. I cry nearly every time. The only balm is seeing the face of the other child. But thank God this is a problem—Thank God, there is still a Colette to come to! I love my "good and perfect gift." She is a treasure.

Speaking of treasures, Colette's ANC is 0.04 today! I asked God for that very number last night...we truly have a God Who hears and answers prayers!

Super Bowl tonight: Eagles vs. Patriots.
PS: TJ got his first real haircut this morning before I left. He looks so much older!

February 5, 2018, Monday   *3.19*
Colette is having her scheduled CT of the abdomen and pelvis right now. It was quite a hassle this morning in preparation. She was NPO [nothing by mouth] at 3:00 AM because the CT was scheduled for 8:30 AM. All was going well. We were headed down

for the procedure when the nurse got a call from the CT technician to see if Colette had received her oral contrast…oral contrast? She hadn't gotten any! So now she needed to get the contrast (which took an hour to run through her NG into her stomach) after which she would need to wait another two hours before it would be safe to put her under general anesthesia! Poor little hungry, tired Colette! We had to do this all in the noisy, chaotic PACU. She was an angel per usual and endured it all without a fuss. Her ANC is 0.06 today—on the rise!

February 6, 2018, Tuesday   *3.20*

    Today has involved less "travel" for Colette and me. She was fussy last evening (and a bit so today) and has needed to be held with her pacifier quite a bit.

    I learned more about the plan for the next couple of days. She had been scheduled to have a new Broviac placed [she needed a double lumen Broviac which would allow her to receive two different medications at the same time; the Broviac she currently had was only a single lumen. She had been too small at the time of it's placement for a double lumen], *but the surgery has been canceled as her ANC is only 0.19 (they needed it to be at least 0.5). The surgery has been rescheduled for the day she returns to the hospital to start round four of chemotherapy (Feb. 19th). She will still have her eye exam tomorrow and a repeat kidney test on Thursday. Hopefully we can go home after the kidney test.*

    I got a large mat from Stephanie (the most wonderful Child Life Specialist imaginable) that we have placed on the floor giving Colette more space to learn to roll. I also asked for another OT consult as we have not made much progress getting Colette to take anything by mouth. After that first bout of interest with solids, she hasn't taken much; and she isn't very interested in the bottle or nursing.

February 9, 2018, Friday   *3.23*

    We are home! Colette had a rapid climb in her ANC (which was such an answer to prayer). Wednesday it was 0.73, and on Thursday it was 1.73! We were discharged after her kidney test on Thursday. The only downside has been Tim and TJ's absence as they both are sick (we do not want to risk Colette getting sick like she did last time she was home!) TJ got to see Colette for a quick moment before he was hurried off like Amy in Little Women *when Beth has Scarlet Fever. I say it lightly, but it was anything but a light matter. Even now, I am pushing it from my mind. Oh, how I miss him! How I miss my family!*

It seems so right that there is snow on the ground—burying my backyard. That is exactly how I feel about my life at the moment. I recognize pieces of it…normal structures like I recognize parts of my backyard. I see the giant tree stump and the remains of my flower garden. Places once filled with sweet memories—once covered with our laughter and foot prints. Now they are all hidden, as if asleep, waiting to re-awaken in spring. So too, one day, the spring will come back to my life. The "snow" of separation will melt, and my house will be our home. Tim, TJ, Colette and I will be here…together. It will be normal for TJ to wake from a nap and see me. Colette will forget that there ever was a world but this one. Her eyes will grow accustomed to opening in a room of cream and blue. How wonderful to look around and see winter but have the power to dream of spring.

February 10, 2018, Saturday   3.24

    Our family is all together again—TJ came through the door with his first words being "Coco?" I <u>love</u> seeing them together. xoxoxoxo She just watches him while he plays all around her. Suddenly, she catches his eye, and he prances over to her to "show" her this or that or just give her a brief pat. Once they were laying side by side playing on a blanket when he suddenly looked over, took her hand and kissed it! How sweet is that love? As a reference point, he doesn't even kiss me spontaneously!

February 12, 2018, Monday   3.26

    It has been glorious being home. Honestly, it is so different from last time. First of all, Colette is SLEEPING! All I have to do is swaddle, give her a pacifier and walk out of the room—she's asleep in a matter of minutes! God has certainly answered that prayer! He seems to have mercifully allowed her to learn to self-soothe and fall asleep effortlessly…such a gift to both mother and child! Secondly, TJ and Colette adore each other! Colette just smiles and smiles at him—bursting into laughter at his silly antics. TJ fetches things for her and talks to her in the sweetest way. He notices every detail about her from her scant little fuzzy hair to a piece of lint on her shirt. The only thing he pays no attention to is her NG. He never asks about it or acknowledges it in any way, which is surprising to me as he is usually so inquisitive about anything amiss. But I guess to him, nothing IS amiss—the NG is just a part of his little friend Colette.

    However blind TJ chooses to be about the NG, Colette does not adhere to such a policy. Yesterday while working on belly time with her Aunt Amy, Colette got a tiny finger under the tape, and out the NG came! We had a brief moment of panic, but as TJ was down for his nap, we took the opportunity to attempt to place a new NG. I got it in without trouble, and it works nicely much to our relief. However, the only spare NG we had available was extremely long! Poor Colette looks like she has a leash attached to her.

Anyway, we had a wonderful day preparing for Valentine's Day. I made cookies with TJ that are covered in "pink and oranges" (TJ's colloquial for M&Ms) as well as Valentine's Day cards. Wonderful day…wonderful memories.

February 14, 2018, Wednesday 3.28

What a sweet Valentine's Day! Yesterday Mom watched TJ while Tim and I took Colette for her check up. Her weight has remained the same since discharge, which they were fine with. Her kidney test results showed that her kidneys were functioning slightly below normal. Dr. Stearns believes this is temporary due to the fact that the chemo she has been receiving is over working her kidneys. The results simply mean that they will need to adjust her chemo doses and get a renal doctor involved to keep an eye on her kidney function in the future.

In the evening, Mom and Dad watched TJ and Colette while Tim and I went out to dinner. We went to the very place we ate when we found out that Colette was going to be a girl! We had a wonderful time.

This morning, workers from Help Me Grow[13] came to start the evaluation process. They will provide assistance with Colette's developmental needs by sending either a PT or an OT to the house while we're home from the hospital. They seem extremely helpful! When the littles wake up from their naps, I have their Valentine treats waiting for them! xoxoxox

PS: Colette's tummy time is improving…she is so close to rolling over!

February 15, 2018, Thursday 3.29

Colette is officially six months old today! Hurray! Abby came over today to play with the littles, and we've been able to go outside (it's in the 50s!)

February 19, 2018, Monday 4.0

What a lovely, sweet time we have had at home. TJ was banished again over the weekend due to another runny nose; Mom and I stayed with Colette. It was glorious being home with Colette—her color improved, her belly time improved (she even tries to push up on her hands while on her belly!) We brought TJ home last night so we could have one last night together. To avoid spreading his germs, we put Colette in her room and closed the door

---

[13] Help Me Grow is an organization that supports early childhood development by providing enrichment therapy to children who are developmentally delayed.

then carried TJ up to his room and closed his door. He was <u>not</u> satisfied with this arrangement and insisted on just one peek at his "Coco" before going to bed. This peek satisfied his brotherly soul, and he went to bed without a fuss.

Unfortunately, for some reason known only to God and himself, TJ woke ready to go at 4:00 AM. He wasn't crying…just singing! Tim and I remained in bed confused and hopeful that this "morning" chorus in the pitch black would end as quickly as it began. Before long, the singing ceased and calls for "Mommy!" and "Coco!" were heard. We then hastily gave him a cup of milk to quiet him, and he went back to bed. Who can understand the ways of a child?

At 6:00 AM, I turned off Colette's overnight feed as she needed to be NPO in preparation for her surgery. By 7:30 AM, Colette, Mom and I were on our way. She had her double lumen Broviac placed with only a slight complication of blood loss that required a transfusion (her red blood cell count had been pretty low to start with).

We got a double room on the oncology floor after the surgery, and we have quickly set up shop. Aside from one episode of pain which was subdued by Tylenol; she is doing well. Mom stayed with her, and I went home for the night. Starting tomorrow, I will be at the hospital indefinitely.

CHAPTER 8

The Fourth Round

F*ebruary 20, 2018, Tuesday*   *4.1*
     *To quote the shirt that Colette is wearing, "The Adventure Begins!" We have
     started round four of chemo. She is getting her two chemotherapy drugs Car-
boplatin and Thiotepa today and tomorrow. The following day will be her one day of rest,
and the stem cell transplant will occur the day after that.*

     *Apparently, this Carboplatin is hard on the ears and causes significant nausea and
vomiting (none so far, but she is on around-the-clock Zofran and Decadron for nausea).
Thiotepa, however, is the beast to be reckoned with. She cannot come in contact with any
plastic while the Thiotepa is in her system (a total of three days) or her skin will develop
second degree burns. For this reason, we are also unable to use any tape on her. Her NG
is out and her Foley and Broviac are being held in place merely by Kerlix gauze wrapped
tightly around her entire trunk making her look like a mummy. We are not allowed to
have any skin to skin contact with her because the Thiotepa is excreted from her body
through the skin. Disposable diapers are also forbidden because they too would create burns
on her skin. Instead, she is sporting a cloth diaper held together by safety pins. Lastly, she
must be showered every six hours for the next three days to remove the chemo from her skin.*

     *In spite of it all, she is doing so well. I am trying to nurse her to keep a little something
in her belly (it's the only way she can get any nutrients because her NG is out), but after I*

finish I have to shower to wash off any trace amounts of chemo that may have gotten on me through her skin. My mom is with me to help with this process, and we have been told to shower and launder any clothes, sheets or linens that have touched Colette every six hours. One can only imagine the amount of laundry these next three days will produce.

It is very difficult to re-adjust to hospital life after being home. The waiting for things…the endless knocks on the door (especially while Colette is <u>trying</u> to sleep). It is hard—so <u>hard</u>—not to be short and angry. I have many people praying for us, and I must trust God's endless mercy and faithfulness because I fail so often. It feels so impossible to be Colette's mom here. There are so many hands touching her, needing to do this or that, cutting her naps short, insisting that x or y would be better for her. I feel so pushed back—so unnecessary. Does she even know me? Oh, how I just want to stand outside her door and say "STOP!" Emptying the sharps container is not important right now, and the garbage cans can overflow for the next hour—just stay out and let my girl sleep.

I can't even kiss her now—I didn't realize how often I kiss her. Every time I pick her up, I go to kiss her on the head and remember—no skin contact! Maybe that's where this rant is coming from—pent up kisses. They must be like the manna God sent to the Israelites—if you store them, they rot [Exodus 16:14-20]! I'm just filled to the brim with rotten kisses, and it is leaving me sick with frustration.

By the grace of God, I am still her mother. He will give me the wisdom and grace I need to be the mom she needs here.

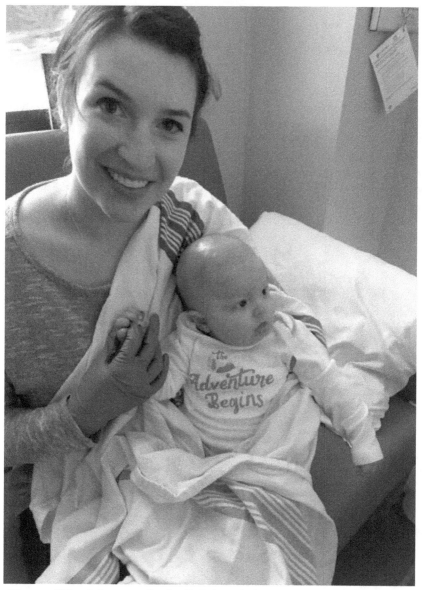

Picture: "The Adventure Begins!" Colette being loved in spite of Thiotepa precautions

February 21, 2018, Wednesday   *4.2*

   Do days really exist here? Wednesday, Sunday, Friday—they are all the same…each one filled with the unexpected, each one unreliable…

   Anyway, we are only four showers away from being done with the Thiotepa precautions (hurray!). It hasn't been worse or better than I expected—just about what I had imagined. Her showers are at 9 AM/3 PM/9 PM/3 AM. My mom and I have quite the routine down. Before the nurses come, we get everything set up: one towel on the floor by the shower to step out on, one towel to the side for Colette, new bed sheets, new chucks pad, new receiving blanket all on the couch ready to be exchanged for the old ones by Mom while I'm showering Colette. We then get scissors and tape ready on the bed for the removal of all the Kerlix gauze holding the Foley and Broviac in place. One sterile pack for the nurses to use for cleaning the Broviac is set out, and a new pacifier is prepared. Finally, masks are provided for all involved.

   Once the gear is gathered, I put on a pair of shorts, flip-flops and a thick chemo gown so that I'm ready to hold Colette in the shower.

   When the nurses come, we (carefully!) cut the Kerlix gauze that is "holding" her Foley in place. I emphasize carefully because the nurse at 3:00 AM accidentally cut right through the Foley when she was cutting the Kerlix which resulted in the need for a new Folly to be placed by two nurses from the PICU (as well as excruciating pain for Colette). I have since taken to cutting the Kerlix myself to avoid such mishaps. After the Foley is free, the Kerlix around the Broviac comes off, and finally the cloth diaper is removed. I then hook her Foley bag to the ties of the chemo gown around my waist, pick Colette up and, while the nurse pushes the IV pole that is attached to Colette, shuffle to the shower. I test the warmth of the water by sticking out a foot before gingerly holding my poor girl out in front of me so that the nurse can spray her down making sure every fold is rinsed carefully.

   At first, Colette would scream wildly, and I would do my best to fight back tears. I kept repeating in my mind the words that Jesus said to Peter in Gethsemane, "Shall I not drink the cup which My Father has given me?" [John 18:11b]. This is the cup God has prepared for Colette. I cannot and will not try to prevent her from drinking it. And it is also the cup He has prepared for me—I must drink it, however bitter.

   While this is going on, Mom is whisking off the old linens and replacing them with new ones.

After the shower, Colette is draped with a towel, and I carry her slowly back to the bed (careful to keep my flip-flop feet on the towel on the floor to prevent the area from getting too wet). Once I lay her down, I reattach the Foley to the bed and skulk off to remove my wet things.

Colette gets dried off and the near impossible task of securing a Foley to her leg without tape is begun. We have found the best method is almost making a diaper out of the Kerlix. My mom (who studied YouTube videos on the process) then exercises her skill in cloth diapering. Finally, the nurse "sterilely" wraps the Broviac, and we put a new onesie over our mummified sweetheart (a onesie with a hole cut into the left armpit to allow for easy temperature taking at naps and nighttime!)

Colette is typically worn out by this time and is merely whimpering with her eyes shut. I hold her or nurse her to calm her down then out she goes for a nap.

My mom and I are almost delirious with exhaustion. At one point, we both laid down for a nap, and about ten minutes in we had a knock on the door. I popped up only to have a volunteer come walking through the door with a dog by her side saying "Oh, do you want to pet the dog?"

Unless the dog was prepared to sing us a lullaby, there could not be two people on the earth less disposed to pet a dog at that moment. We could not stop laughing…still can't!

Colette is doing well for the most part. Her skin is dry, red and sensitive. She is on oxycodone and Tylenol as needed which seems to be needed around-the-clock. She isn't playful—just sleepy and needing to be held and we are happy to oblige.

Also, she gave us a scare with her heart rate. It kept dipping into the 60s while she slept, but an EKG showed that all was well.

One more day!

February 22, 2018, Thursday   *4.3*

One more shower to go! We made it through another night with no major mishaps— only an unfortunate wet diaper just after we finished wrapping her up in Kerlix!

Mom and I are definitely in a state of delirium. To quote her, "I feel like a rag…an old, gray, dirty, wrinkled rag." I can't say enough how thankful I am for her. She never stops—up to get a pacifier in the middle of the night, rocking Colette till her legs are numb (not to mention other areas of her anatomy), cleaning this, organizing that—all while maintaining a life-saving sense of humor. Without her it would be miserable; with her, it is misery seasoned with a smile.

Tim has also been glorious. He took two weeks off work to be with TJ, and he has sent me so many pictures and videos as well as the most detailed updates on TJ. Texts from him are like little snippets of heaven.

A woman was here earlier in the week from Palliative Care, and she was enquiring as to how I am coping with difficulty. I answered that I am coping beautifully with difficulty. I have God (the God of all comfort) and an incredible family.

February 23, 2018, Friday   *Stem Cell Transplant Day 4.4*

Colette is officially off her Thiotepa precautions! It is glorious to simply pick her up and kiss her sweet, soft head once more! She did beautifully through it all. She has just been mildly fussy, and her skin is quite red and sensitive.

Aunt Amy and McLaine were ready to take over the roles of chief snugglers at 5:00 yesterday evening, and I got home around 6:00. TJ…xoxoxoxoxo all evening! He had a wonderful time with Daddy, but how I ached for him. I ACHE to be his mom again. I want him to wake up from a nap and call for me…not a long list of people who may or may not be out there. I long for him to know, "Mom put me down; Mom will get me up." But again, this is the cup my good Father has prepared for Tim, TJ, Colette and I. How can I doubt it is for the best?

I went back to the hospital at 10:00 this morning—Stem Cell Transplant Day!
It only took seven minutes for the transplant! The process that involves so much detailed preparation is rather anticlimactic in the final step. Two nurses came in carrying the syringe full of stem cells (which looked just like regular blood). Once Colette was attached to the cardiac monitor, the nurses merely attached the syringe to her Broviac and slowly pushed in the life-saving stem cells. The nurse said it was the easiest transplant she has ever done. Colette slept through the first half! She didn't have any change to her vital signs or any vomiting (which is unheard of apparently).

She was only mildly irritable but calmed down with Tylenol. It sounds like the next week to ten days will be rough. I went home to be with TJ and Tim for one final evening so I can devote all of next week to Colette. Planning on returning tomorrow.

February 24, 2018, Saturday   *4.5*

I'm back in Colette Land. TJ and Tim are at Hocking Hills for the big Ferguson family reunion [my mom's family]—*how fun for them!*

As for the little princess, she is doing well. She had one episode of gagging/vomiting but nothing else since. She has, however, struggled with diarrhea (throw-out-the-onesie type diarrhea). I have been told that this is the start of mucositis [a painful condition caused by chemotherapy in which the entire digestive tract develops painful ulcers making it difficult to eat and drink as well as causing vomiting and terrible diarrhea; we were told to expect this side effect with the final three rounds of chemotherapy]. *She is really doing so well in spite of it all.*

McLaine left this afternoon as she has to work tonight, but Aunt Amy will be staying to help me. They both have been simply marvelous. Aunt Amy is so cheerful and wonderful with Colette, and McLaine is the best helper. If the greatest is the one who serves, then she is the greatest [Matt. 23:11]. *There is never anything too low or too tiring or too monotonous. I love them both. I love Tim for taking TJ three hours away to my family reunion. I love all the people that have been supplying Tim and TJ with meals. I love every person who has taken the time to send a card or say a prayer on our behalf. I love all these glorious heroes God has surrounded me with.*

February 26, 2018, Monday   *4.7*

Colette continues to do well. Yesterday, she grew finicky with her pacifier and wouldn't take it for her first nap which resulted in a nap in the swing, but by the evening she was taking it again which was a great relief. She also has had more vomiting. Still, she is so cheery and lovely.

The past few days have been major snuggle days, and I've been able to study her darling face. Her eyelashes are completely gone now and only two little patches of light hair make up her eyebrows. If anything, the loss of hair has made her beautiful eyes more mesmerizing. Oh, the glory of rocking her—eyes fixed on one another, inches apart. To have her grasping tightly to my finger, head perfectly nestled in my arm—I can see her now! Those magnificent, unblinking eyes, the little pacifier occasionally bobbing up and down as she remembers to suck—a treasure in the darkness.

She slept well last night. She went down at 9:30 PM and, besides being woken by the nurse at 5:00 AM for her daily lab draws, vital sign check and weight check, she slept peacefully until 8:00 AM. McLaine has returned to help. Tim and TJ are back home from Hocking Hills with pictures and videos that testify to a wonderful time. I am looking forward to seeing my boys.

February 27, 2018, Tuesday 4.8

The mucositis vomiting has definitely picked up; however, she still has no signs of pain. We've added Benadryl to her regimen for nausea.

She remains pleasant, snuggly and wonderful. Mom came to be with Colette so now I'm home with my boys. Big plans to enjoy the sun and 50 degree weather outside!
PS: Big drop in ANC today which was expected

February 28, 2018, Wednesday 4.9

Last day of February—what a fast month! TJ, Tim and I had a fun morning. We went to the library for story time, although TJ didn't last too long due to the draw of the train table in the children's section. We got some books and a "Monkey George" and "Stuffins" (Curious George and Doc Mcstuffins) DVD which thrilled TJ. Then we went to the Parma Metroparks where we enjoyed a wee bit of nature before the rain sent us home. Now it is time for a nap.

Being home with TJ just makes me want to count the weeks till we will all be home again…be content!

Anyway, Colette vomited a couple times today per mom's report. The plan is to add Ativan around-the-clock to see if it helps with the nausea.

March 2, 2018, Friday 4.11

Yesterday was an eventful day. I took over Colette's care around 11:00 AM, and my mom left around noon. Colette was scheduled to have a new NG placed due to the fact that she had vomited out her old one. She also needed platelets.

The transfusion started just after my mom left and, nearing its finish, I noticed that her arms were shaking. I asked the nurse about it (wondering if she was having a seizure). She told me that she was having rigors [a sudden shaking, accompanied by a rise in temperature that can occur with blood transfusions] *from the transfusion and called for the doctor. Her temperature rose as did her heart rate. Colette herself grew very pale and looked just plain sick. I held her until the rigors stopped. The attending doctor ordered an IV fluid bolus to bring down her heart rate, as well as cultures and some antibiotics. The bolus seemed to do the trick, and Colette was soon looking more normal, much to my relief.*

I held her for the rest of the day, and although she did spike another fever in the evening, she was calm. Her feeds were stopped completely because her vomiting has increased even with the medications. We hope to resume the NG feeds once her stomach has had time to settle.

Today she has had more normal vital signs and has tolerated the tiny bits of milk she has gotten by nursing. Mostly she has just been groggy and sleepy.

Mom's on her way to take over tonight while I spend the weekend with the boys. ANC still 0.

March 3, 2018, Saturday   4.12

Colette is doing so well per the update from Mom. No nausea or vomiting, and her temperature is back to normal. No need for any blood transfusions, and no need for any pain medicine!

As for the boys and I, we have been having a glorious day together. We made TJ's crib into Noah's Ark, complete with stuffed animals. TJ's favorite part is "building" the ark with all his toy tools. We also enjoyed sledding down Memphis Hill and took a hike along the river. It's beautifully sunny but cold outside. There was just enough snow to sled.

March 4, 2018, Sunday   4.13

We were able to go to church, which was the first time in quite a while. That is another thing I long for—the regularity of going to church. It is so strange that what was once so natural and routine is now the exception. But those days will come again…

Meanwhile, Colette got platelets and had no reaction this time. She is pale with a higher heart rate than normal—I suspect a low red blood count in the morning. The big news is…ANC 0.12! Home soon?

March 5, 2018, Monday 4.14

Colette has been pretty uncomfortable. She spent the majority of the day in my arms, which is not something that I resent in any way. But poor girl! Oxycodone has been scheduled, and the dose has been increased. Hopefully that will relieve her pain. Her NG feeds have been increased as she has been tolerating them better.

Her ANC is 0.54! So thrilled about that—must go, little girl is calling!

March 6, 2018, Tuesday 4.15

Vomiting has increased again…hopefully only temporarily. She slept most of the day in my arms. There weren't many wake periods but plenty of cuddles. Her ANC is 2.31! Tomorrow they hope to stop the Neupogen shot which she is getting daily once again in order to stimulate bone marrow growth. Once they confirm that her ANC will remain up even without the shot (and once her pain and nausea/vomiting are under control) she can go home!

March 7, 2018, Wednesday 4.16

Her ANC is 5.6! How's that for an ANC? The only thing keeping us here is her nausea and vomiting. She didn't vomit yesterday so the plan is to slowly increase her feeds. If she tolerates her feeds today, they will wean her off the Ativan. They also want to stop the oxycodone today as she is no longer getting Neupogen (so theoretically, no more bone pain).

She has started rubbing her eyes quite a bit today, and they are rather red and swollen. The doctors wonder if she is having some type of drug allergy.

PS: SHE ROLLED OVER!

March 8, 2018, Thursday 4.17

Every day the chords between my heart and Colette's grow tighter—when I'm alone with her they seem to choke me. Oh, Colette do you know how incredible you are? Do you realize how other-worldly you are? You are an angel—a strong, gentle, patient little sufferer. How are you so good? I see your tiny, new eyelashes starting to appear. They are shooting out so quietly, evidence of your determined, gentle, little soul. I adore you. God has truly made you a special, special girl; and I am so thankful to have had you so long, sweet one.

March 10, 2018, Saturday   *4.19*

    I thought we would be going home today, but Colette's eyelid redness is keeping us here. Such a disappointment as there is almost certainly nothing wrong with her eyes! The redness is just above and below her eyes and comes and goes throughout the day. We were all set to go today, but at the last minute the resident consulted with an eye doctor who examined Colette and insisted that she stay for a couple of days of observation to rule out a virus! I am so disappointed. I haven't felt so down and unsettled in a long time.

PS: God is sovereign, I know.

March 13, 2018, Tuesday   *4.22*

    We are home! We came home Sunday, and it has been go, go, go! Even now, I'm writing while on hold with the pharmacy company trying to get Colette's medicine ordered, and such a funny thing happened. While I was on hold, I was accidentally connected to another person who was also trying to order something! We had a good laugh then hung up to redial our orders.

    Anyway, Colette has done pretty well since being home, but today she seems a trifle fussier. The nights have been hard—to quote Tim, "I can't believe we survived the night...and it's only Monday!" But her eye redness cleared up without any difficulty, which is a relief. She had her evaluation for Help Me Grow, and the evaluator was pleased with her development. The biggest delay she has is in eating, so an OT will be working with her while she is at home.

March 14, 2018, Wednesday   *4.23*

    Things have gotten quite difficult with Colette. Yesterday, she did fine in the morning but got more agitated as the day went on. By the time Tim came home, I had to hold her to keep her calm. She went down at eight that night only to wake about forty-five minutes later. This became the pattern for the night. She was up nearly every hour requiring rocking, walking and patting. I gave her something for gas and then something for pain which seemed to help, but not majorly. TJ got up once as well (it obviously seemed like the thing to do), and I had to pump at one point during the night. In the end, it was a long night.

    This morning she vomited and still is not her normal self. I wonder if perhaps she's having trouble with withdrawal from all the medicines she was on while in the hospital.

    Anyway, what a night! How I cried! Tears of exhaustion and of anger—not at her, never at her. I tried so hard to keep my mind thinking right—God's sovereignty, it's just one night, etc. But the tears flowed fast as did my temper. It is the most incredible thing—

the longing to go, to run. Over and over I wanted to bolt out of the house and find some quiet place to collapse and cry and cry and then sleep. I wanted it so badly. Still, the urge <u>*NEVER*</u> *overpowers the chain keeping me here. The chain of love for TJ and Colette. The very thought of them wanting and needing me, and me being selfishly absent—of them crying for me, their mommy, and me not being here to comfort them—shatters every urge to run. No prison bars could ever be stronger than those comprised of a mother's love. God makes a mother's love so strong that it even triumphs over the seemingly all-powerful self-love. It is a very good thing because nothing else could convince a free, independent being to submit to a completely dependent, demanding little being. Talk about a constraining love!*

March 15, 2018, Thursday   4.24

Colette has started to improve. Little by little she is becoming more like herself. She has been content playing alone and is waking from naps chatty and not tearful. Hurray for our little Colette!

Meanwhile, today was momentous because Colette had her hearing screen and weekly check-up. At her check-up, she received pentamidine (an IV antibiotic given every two weeks for the prevention of a particular type of pneumonia she is vulnerable to as a transplant patient). During the infusion, she instantly had a terribly stuffy nose that wouldn't allow her to suck on her pacifier! The poor darling was irate! I went for the nurse to ask for saline drops for her nose only to find out that stuffiness was a possible side effect of the medicine. She was given Benadryl and eventually settled back down to sleep in my arms with the cutest little snore imaginable.

After this (and after getting her labs drawn…all of which looked good), she went to the PACU where she was prepped and put to sleep for the hearing screen. It came back PERFECT! No hearing loss at all! PRAISE GOD for His protection! She's snoozing now but is otherwise well.

March 17, 2018, Saturday   4.26

Yesterday was an exciting day. Tim led his "team" for a fundraising event for St. Baldrick's [a childhood cancer research charity] *in which he shaved his head! They raised over two thousand dollars for pediatric cancer research and ended up being one of the top three fundraisers in our area. The shaving was done at Rainbow, and Tim and I took TJ to the event (Mom stayed home with Colette). It was amazing seeing so many people shaving their heads. The one that stood out to me the most was a woman probably in her 60s with long grey hair who walked in alone and went right up to one of the barber chairs and sat down—full of pride and firmness. The woman was asked if she wanted to donate hair (cut off about 10 inches) or donate and shave. She replied "Donate and shave" with such joy, and again, such pride. She chatted with those near her but was out of my hearing. Later, TJ and I were standing towards the back when she came up, head freshly shaved, and started talking with TJ. We chatted a bit then I told her how much I admired what she did.*

"I do it every two years," she replied, "in honor of my daughter." Aghh, I'm tearing up writing this. But there were no tears in her eyes—just the f iercest pride. She told me her daughter, Faith, was diagnosed at eleven with ovarian cancer and that they had fought for four years before she died. Oh, the pain! She then said to my pitying response of sorrow,

"It's all right—I know where she is. She is with her other sister, and she is all right now!"

Her other daughter, it seems, died of spina bifida at two-and-a-half months! How much sorrow can a woman bear? I told her about Colette, and only then did she begin to cry. We cried together—two mothers with a sisterhood of fear and sorrow. It was incredible to feel it. I wanted to cling to her, to ask her a million questions because she KNOWS. No one else in the room may know—they may sympathize, but she has been there. She has had her 3:00 AM vigil of terror. And what is more, she has walked further down the road of pain than I pray God will ever ask me to walk. I will never forget looking into her dark brown empathetic eyes. We held each other for a moment. She told me it took her eight years to rise again, to live again; but that she did and does live now.

Oh God, may I never have to walk those footsteps. Please, let Colette live!

Picture: Colette admiring her daddy's shaved head following the
St. Baldrick's fundraiser.

March 20, 2018, Tuesday 4.29

Today has been simply lovely…could it be because Colette is sleeping well again? I think so! Dr. Stearns put her on around-the-clock oxycodone at her last appointment, and it has turned things around beautifully for Colette. She is content and playful when awake and sleeps without waking in pain! She still has trouble around feeding times but hopefully the new medicine she was started on for acid reflux will make a difference.

I've been alone with TJ and Colette all morning, and although it has been a little crazy, it has mostly been lovely. I feel like a mom again—queen of my little castle, and it is glorious! I will enjoy it, however brief my reign is.

March 22, 2018, Thursday 4.31

Yesterday turned out to be quite a long day! While TJ went to Grammy's, Tim and I left for Rainbow a little after 7:00 AM for Colette's kidney function test which was scheduled for 8:00 AM. We were tucked in a little hold of a room in the basement that we attempted to clean with the infamous "purple wipes" [Rainbow used a particular type of antiseptic wipes for cleaning that we referred to lovingly as the "purple wipes"; we never quite felt safe until we had donned gloves (the wipes were so potent that they could not come in contact with skin) and cleansed any room Colette entered with the purple wipes!] *Colette was an angel. The test involved a series of blood draws at specific time intervals after Colette had been injected with a dye-type substance (draws at 5 min./10 min./15 min./30 min./2 hours/45 min/45 min). Colette slept most of the time in my arms while I watched an incredible documentary on the Roosevelts! Tim got us lunch around noon, and for the two hour break we went up to the outpatient clinic so Colette's labs could be drawn and vital signs and weight could be taken before her appointment at 1:00 that afternoon. Colette did vomit once and had an unexpected diaper explosion leaving us in the very vulnerable position of having no extra outfits. But she made it!*

After the kidney test was finished, we took her back upstairs to complete her outpatient appointment. Her lab work came back showing that her red blood cell count was low. That, combined with the fact that her heart rate was a touch high, led to the decision to give her a blood transfusion. This meant an admission to the oncology floor as it was getting too late in the day to do a transfusion in the outpatient clinic.

Tim left to find us some dinner while Colette and I settled down in Mac 6020. She did beautifully with the infusion and was discharged upon its completion. We got home around 9:30 PM. I ushered her up to bed, then collapsed into mine as well.

Today, Tim had parent/teacher conferences from 8:00 AM-8:00 PM. Meanwhile, I met Mary the OT that will be working with Colette through Help Me Grow while we are here at home. She seems wonderful! The goal is to help Colette reach some of the developmental milestones she should be achieving as a seven month old. The focus at first will be to get Colette to eat by mouth, to sit independently and to take liquid from a sippy cup.

March 23, 2018, Friday   *4.32*

    Tim is officially on Spring Break! He will be home the next two weeks to be with TJ as we start round five. It has been so nice being home. While TJ was napping yesterday and my mom was with Colette, I ran to the store. I fell in love with all things spring. I got a beautiful cherry blossom wreath for the door and a tall brown wooden rabbit for the mantle. I love the little chap!

March 26, 2018, Monday   *4.35*

    We have had a bit of an eventful weekend. On Saturday Colette vomited with her first feed, but did better with her subsequent feeds (after a dose of Zofran and Benadryl for nausea). She also had two nose bleeds on the side of her NG. A call to the oncology doctor resulted in the suggestion that the NG be removed and a new one placed through the other side of her nose. Tim and I did as we were told, carefully placing a new NG. All went well, and she did great that night. However, she became terribly fussy with her first two bolus feeds in the morning. By the third she could only make it to an ounce before crying miserably. By the fourth feed, I gave the oncology doctor another call and was told to bring Colette to the ER so she could be evaluated.

    Kayla came to take TJ to Poppa and Oma's while Tim and I packed and brought her to the ER. An x-ray showed the NG to be a little deep. They readjusted the length (pulling it out about 3 cm), and since then Colette has tolerated her feeds beautifully! Because it was already Sunday evening and Colette was scheduled to start chemo the next day, the doctor decided to admit her.

    So we are back on Mac 6—preparing for chemo that will start tomorrow. Colette is napping now; the calm before the storm—they will place the Foley soon.

    I plan on leaving once the Foley is in and she has calmed. It will be my last night home before the four-day stretch.

CHAPTER 9

The Fifth Round

I remember one night during the first round of chemotherapy, laying on the hospital cot after getting up to take Colette's 3:00 AM vital signs. She was tucked back into a sound sleep, but I was wide awake, filled with terror.

My mom was with me that night, and I remember telling her through my tears, "Don't you see, if God is going to demonstrate His power through Colette, He has to take us into some difficult places. It won't be smooth sailing—there is darkness ahead." I was paralyzed by fear.

My mom, in her wisdom, advised me not to borrow trouble. There was no cause to shed tears for a sorrow that had not yet unfolded. If and when the darkness came, God would meet us there and bear us through.

The fifth round of chemotherapy became the unfolding of this fear. God began the process of a gradual descent, a drift downward into darker and darker territories. Colette's seven-month-old body had undergone such extreme medical treatment, and this fifth round of chemotherapy seemed to be her breaking point.

For this reason, the next two months of journal entries will contain rather detailed medical information. For some, it will be as incomprehensible as it is undesired. For others, it will be a compelling tale of a tiny body fighting for life. I wrestled greatly over how much detail to leave in, knowing that the two camps of readers would want varying levels of information. I leave the medical details for those who desire it, and encourage those who do not to merely skim to their hearts desire. The Appendix A in the back of the book provides a chart of normal vital signs for a child Colette's age.

However, please do not let the depth or the detail of the next two months cause you to shy away from the material. These months were pivotal in our journey. It was during them that we traveled through the land of valleys. We had grown accustomed to living in the Valley of Fear. It had actually become bearable through that radiant beam of light in the distance called Hope. We were now to enter new and deeper valleys: the Valley of Terror and the Valley of Despair. Valleys so deep that the rays of Hope rarely penetrated the gloom. We walked in dread through these valleys, for we were aware that around any bend could lie the deepest valley, the Valley of the Shadow of Death. So, I urge you to continue on. Use the medical information only as it is helpful to you, but walk with us. Come see the valleys where the Lord led us, then watch as the glorious dawn of Hope breaks through, declaring us victorious.

March 27, 2018, Tuesday   5.0

Were I making this entry an hour ago, it would certainly have a different tone; however I am writing now, after Colette has had morphine…now that she's kicking her little feet around and blowing raspberries!

Last evening, she had her Foley placed by the urologist; and even though it was the easiest insertion yet, Colette was still very sensitive afterwards. I made sure that Colette and my mom were comfortable before leaving around 6:30 PM. All was well in the early evening, but apparently the night got worse. She was up for hours at a time crying. By the time I arrived in the morning, poor Mom was struggling to manage Colette who was entangled by her Foley, NG feed (hooked to an IV pole) and two seperate IV infusions. Not a one-woman job! Especially under Thiotepa precautions! [Colette was once more receiving Thiotepa which required the special precautions previously mentioned (no direct skin contact, no diapers or tape and showers every six hours).] *I brought TJ and a coffee to cheer Oma while I resumed snuggling with Colette.*

From the time of my arrival, Colette had to be held constantly with a pacifier to keep her tears tolerably at bay. Any movement seemed to cause her excruciating pain. By 3:00

PM, I asked that she be given something stronger than Tylenol. She then received morphine and in ten minutes, Colette the Delightful was restored to us! She has been chatty and playful ever since.

Other than that, all is well.

March 28, 2018, Wednesday   5.1

Only four more showers! Thiotepa precautions are no easy business!

March 29, 2018, Thursday   5.2

What a horrible night! To quote Mom, "I feel like I've been run over by a truck…and Colette was driving!"

Colette didn't go down until around 11:00 PM then was up at 12:30 AM crying harder than I've heard yet. It was melt-down central in Mac 6011. In the end, she got Tylenol and my mom and I took turns rocking her until her 3:00 AM shower. You can imagine my mental state. To be honest, I feel as though I should have been awarded the world's worst mom award. But Colette did a little better after her shower, requiring only one pacifier run from 4:00 AM till 9:00 AM. The last shower is in less than two hours which is a thing to rejoice over.

On a side note, in rounds this morning a resident doctor gave an update on Colette saying, "So besides a little fussiness, Colette did very well last night." I wanted to slap his well-rested cheek. Just kidding! Sort of.

March 30, 2018, Friday   5.3

What a day! We finished Colette's showers yesterday around 3:00 PM. My mom left exhausted while McLaine took her post. Things went well until I took Colette's vitals at 5:00 PM. Her heart rate was 160s with a blood pressure of 60s over 30s. She was well looking, but the vital signs wouldn't clear up. I got the nurse, who got the resident, who got the fellow and attending doctors. After watching her for about an hour and giving her a bolus of IV fluids, Colette's blood pressure returned to near normal ranges and remained so through the night.

This morning, Colette was very sleepy but did well with her stem cell transplant (no nausea/vomiting). Her blood pressures and heart rates were steady at first, but then began to change. Her heart rate went up to 160s-170s while her blood pressure fell to 60s over 30s again. Then it dropped to 50s over 20s. The doctors again assembled in the room and *went back and forth as to what should be done until the nurse (Leslee, a favorite) called a PACT.*

Colette remained very sleepy this entire time. The PICU fellow and nurse who arrived minutes later in response to the PACT evaluated Colette and had her transferred to the PICU.

It took some time, but her blood pressures and heart rates eventually returned to normal ranges. Her last heart rate was in the 140s and her blood pressure was 90/63...all is well!

March 31, 2018, Saturday   *5.4*

Colette returned to the oncology floor today. Her heart rate is still elevated, but her blood pressures are stable. Vomiting began today, and her pain continues. She has been switched to continuous feeds with Benadryl, Zofran and Ativan for nausea, and she gets morphine for pain.

She must feel terrible. She is so swollen from all the fluids she got yesterday when her blood pressures were low, and all the medications she is getting are making her pretty sleepy. All in all, she just looks sick, which is hard to see.

I can't even think about TJ. I miss him so badly it hurts inside, but I can't leave my girl.

April 1, 2018, Sunday   *Easter 5.5*

Christ is risen! Last night was one dark, sad night. Colette—oh, she breaks my heart—is so lethargic. Her poor little eyes. Even when she is awake (which isn't often), her eyes seem so tired but so wise. She looks at you as if she knows this is so wrong*—life should not be this way. Last night I held her for hours while she slept or calmly stared into my face.*

She began having trouble maintaining high enough oxygen saturation levels in the evening, so she was placed on oxygen (1/2 liter). They did a chest x-ray around 11:00 PM to make sure no infection or fluid accumulation was behind her drop in oxygen levels. The x-ray came back looking good. Still, she needed another fluid bolus in the middle of the night to help her maintain high enough blood pressures.

I was also troubled last night by the thought of TJ. I ached for him. I grieved over our splintered family! Needless to say, there was a lot of sadness last night. But I think, for the first time, I realized the incredible truth about Easter. Because of Easter, because Jesus Christ rose from the dead, the end of the story will be a good one. <u>There will not be a bad ending</u> in spite of these bad chapters. Whatever happens to Colette, whatever lies ahead for me, a thousand years from now I will be smiling because He will have made all things right. The death, burial, and resurrection of Jesus Christ has opened the door for me to have peace with God and has struck down the terror of death and separation. Death has become merely the doorway to something infinitely more glorious. One day I will look back on these days as a "watch in the night." Beauty awaits us! These thoughts were the turning point for me last night.

Tim and TJ came in the morning to hunt for the Easter eggs and Easter baskets that the staff had hidden in the room. It was wonderful until they had to leave. I walked TJ and Tim out to the car, trying to capture every last second with them. When we got to the car, TJ cried, "Mommy coming? Sit here!" I had a rather tearful walk from the garage back to the room. But back I went to where my little sleepy darling lay. There will be better days than this.

So far Colette's vital signs have been normal today. She remains very lethargic and has vomited twice. The attending doctor requested that a T2Turbo MRI [a scan that could be done faster than a traditional MRI and did not require Colette to be under general anesthesia] *be done on Colette tonight or tomorrow to check for fluid collecting in her brain causing hydrocephalus. Her vomiting and lethargy are most likely due to the effects of chemo; however, the doctor doesn't want to overlook the possibility of hydrocephalus.*

Kayla and my parents have arrived to celebrate the day with Colette and I. I'll go home after the MRI to see the boys.

Picture: The darkest Easter, Colette nestled in the arms of her Oma

April 2, 2018, Monday 5.6

Colette's MRI results looked perfect! No changes in the ventricles, no signs of regrowth and the entire brain looks more filled out! Praise God! Her heart rates and blood pressures are back to normal as well which is a relief. However, she still is requiring oxygen, and a new mystery has surfaced. During her routine labs, her blood sugar level came back low requiring her to receive dextrose [an IV infusion of sugar]. Dr. Stearns is unsure of the reason for this so she will continue to be monitored.

For now, I'm home, and it is a beautiful (but cold) sunny day! We plan to spend the morning at the Rocky River Metroparks…how glorious to feel the sun!

April 4, 2018, Wednesday 5.8

Yesterday morning, Colette continued to have low blood sugar levels (in the 50s) [normal levels are 70-100]; I left TJ with Grammy to go see what was going on. When I arrived, Colette seemed sleepy but otherwise normal. The endocrine team came to examine her but only had theories as to the cause of the low blood sugars.

While this was going on, the side room which we had been sleeping in developed a leak in the ceiling! We were told that we needed to move to another room. We gathered our things and shuffled down the hall to another room only to be told later in the evening that another double room had opened up and was available should we desire it. Like all good nomads, we certainly desired more lush nesting grounds and would travel to obtain them! For the second time that day we gathered and stuffed our belongings onto carts and wheelchairs and made our way to the double room. Aunt Amy was with me and assisted in the process (not only with her helpful hands but also with her cheerful heart!).

Today has been a "hold you" day to use a TJ phrase. Colette's red blood cell count was low requiring a transfusion. She is pale, sleepy and a bit more fussy. Aunt Amy and I have taken turns rocking her. As for her blood sugar, it remains unstable; and the mystery remains as to why.

April 5, 2018, Thursday 5.9

Oh, how I want Colette to live! How can you adore someone—hold them so close, stare into their eyes, inches away—and not feel your heart shattering because you <u>know</u> you can do nothing to keep them. I have no power—I have no control. I know no words that can describe how horribly helpless I feel. On nights like tonight I just pray God doesn't ask it of me. These are the words of my blind, panic-stricken heart. But my mind replies: <u>His grace</u> will be sufficient. It will be enough. I will not break; I will not be overcome. I will be sustained by a Rock that is higher than I. He will bear me, comfort me, sustain me. He *will be the lifter of my head. Therefore, I will not fear. Though the seas roar, though the mountains are moved into the midst of them* [Psalms 46]. *All events that are to come are being orchestrated by my Father. My good, loving, all-wise, all-powerful Father Who has known me and has loved me before time began.*

My heart slows now into calm peacefulness…because my mind is stayed on Him. I will trust in the Lord forever.

April 6, 2018, Friday   5.10

Colette is doing well. All her vital signs are normal, and the morphine seems to keep her comfy without causing too much sleepiness. The only issue continues to be her blood sugar! Yesterday she had two blood sugar readings under 50; today she has already had one of 57. No one seems to know why. Mom took over at the hospital while I came home for a weekend with the boys. Looking forward to it for sure!

April 7, 2018, Saturday   5.11

We had a fun morning! We went to see Kevin and Lyssa's new home. They are now less than ten miles away, which is wonderful! They have a pool in the back which whispers alluring prophecies of future fun for all the little ones! TJ and his cousin Miller had a grand time which inevitably led to tears on the way home.

As for Colette, my mom tells me she is having a more difficult day. She pulled out her NG resulting in a traumatic reinsertion (that led to a vomiting episode). She has also been more fussy, requiring her pacifier and quite a bit of snuggling. Perhaps the start of the Neupogen bone pain. Blood sugar levels have been all over but nothing critically low. Still no answers about that. She will be getting a platelet transfusion later today.

April 10, 2018, Tuesday   5.14

Hello from the PICU! What a shock the past couple of days have been.

Sunday started so well. Tim, TJ and I went to church, and afterwards I put TJ down for a nap and came to take over at the hospital. Colette slept most of the day (aside from one chatty period when her favorite resident Allison came to see her). In the evening, her heart rates increased to the upper 160s-170s, and her pulse ox dropped to the low 90s. She was examined and deemed well but was put on a continuous monitor and ½ liter oxygen. I stayed near her overnight, and she remained stable. She slept until 11:00 Monday morning (in spite of vital sign checks and Accu-Chek pokes [skin pricks to check blood sugar levels]) and appeared to be doing well.

In rounds, it was decided to start TPN and lipids [an IV infusion of nutritional needs] *as she has not been able to receive sufficient nutrients through her NG for weeks now. They also decided to attempt to wean her off the oxygen.*

The wean was not successful, and when she woke from her nap, she was inconsolable. She was given a dose of morphine but remained an arching, screaming bundle in my arms. Palliative Care [a branch of the medical team devoted specifically to pain and symptom management] *arrived and increased her morphine dose, but it became an all-day struggle trying to get her comfortable.*

As the day waxed on, the blood pressure battle began. Blood pressures were steadily 60s/30s even after multiple fluid boluses. Eventually, a couple 40s over 20s appeared which resulted in a transfer to PICU bed 1.

We arrived in the PICU around 6:00 PM, and the evening was spent rocking and walking with her while the seemingly impossible task of setting up her TPN, lipids, dextrose, morphine, Narcan, and Vancomycin IV lines was undertaken by an old favorite PICU nurse Catherine. Her blood pressures were 60s/30s but gradually rose overnight while pain management continued to be a problem.

A PICU definition of a "good night" has nothing to do with sleep quality or quantity; therefore, it can be reported that we had a good night. Colette's pain, the night nurse's physiological inability to whisper and unforgiving OCD desire to straighten every tube going to Colette robbed McLaine and I of the sleep that the melatonin we took so desperately desired to give us. The length of these sentences demonstrates my growing sleepless insanity.

We are waiting now for rounds to see if we can return to Mac 6026 today.

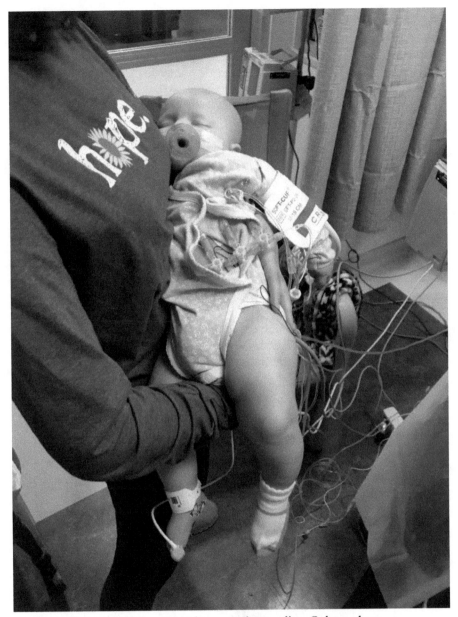

Picture: Holding on to hope, and snuggling Colette close

April 11, 2018, Wednesday   5.15

 Colette was able to return to the oncology floor around 6:00 yesterday evening. She is still struggling with low blood pressures, but they are not as low as before. Her pain continues, but adjustments on her PCA pump [an IV pump that supplied Colette with a constant infusion of pain medicine] *have finally resulted in some smiles! She still requires oxygen and has started to sound congested; but otherwise, she appears much improved.*

 I was able to go home last night once Colette was comfortable, and I've spent a glorious day with TJ-No Pants ("No Pants" he implores! And really, who needs them?)
PS: Her ANC is 1.02

April 14, 2018, Saturday   5.18

 So much to catch up on! Thursday morning, Tim and I dropped TJ off with Kevin and Lyssa before heading to the hospital. We arrived around 10:30 in the morning; Colette was asleep. My mom had told me that Colette had begun having retractions in her chest overnight [inward pulling of the skin between the ribs that occurs when a person is struggling to get enough oxygen] *and had become increasingly congested. Her pulse ox was mid 90s with 1 liter of oxygen. The doctors had been monitoring her but believed that she was still oxygenating well.*

 My mom left shortly after our arrival, and I kept a close eye on Colette while she slept. Soon I noticed nasal flaring [another sign of difficulty breathing] *as well as an increase in the retractions. Her pulse ox then began dipping into the low 90s.*

 When I called for the nurse and the doctor, they were alarmed. They increased her oxygen and sent for the respiratory therapist, but the pulse ox continued to drop, now into the 80s. They tossed ideas back and forth about croup, congestion from mucositis, RSV, etc. The respiratory therapist did some deep suctioning [suctioning of the nose and throat with a lubricated tube in order to remove any secretions blocking the airway] *which caused Colette to cough and then vomited. It seemed to help a bit, but because of her low platelets there was also quite a bit of blood.*

 A nurse then administered racemic epinephrine and a steroid to reduce any inflammation that was potentially blocking the airway. After this, Colette calmed in my arms and was able to maintain a pulse ox in the upper 90s on just 2 liters of oxygen. The doctors dispersed, and the respiratory therapist made arrangements to check on Colette every four hours.

Unfortunately, Colette did not make it to the first four-hour mark before she started dropping her oxygen saturations again and was placed on 3 liters of oxygen. Once more, the oxygen seemed to be ineffective. The doctors returned, and a PACT was called. The fellow from the PICU (Liz who has the amazing ability of lowering my anxiety level by simply entering the room) came and examined her. Deep nasal suctioning was ordered, but this time, the suctioning did not help (poor Colette was beside herself throughout the whole ordeal). Liz, the fellow, then decided to transfer Colette to the PICU.

Upon her arrival in the PICU, Colette looked poorly. She had a lot of retractions and a pulse ox that dropped into the 70s when she cried. A chest x-ray showed fluid in her lungs which led to Lasix immediately being started [a medicine that increases urine output thus reducing the amount of fluid in the body, particularly in the lungs]. *She was also put on high flow oxygen* [a method of delivering oxygen through a stiff rubber nasal tube; the amount of oxygen delivered is much higher in volume and concentration than through a traditional nasal cannula (which Colette had been using)].

Pulmonary and Infectious Disease doctors were consulted. The doctors theorized about some type of infection and wanted to intubate Colette to get a sample of the fluid in her lungs. Things were rough until around 9:00 PM when she suddenly had a major turnaround. She became more alert and her breathing seemed more settled. They were able to avoid intubating her. The night of no sleep for Tim and I (well, three hours of sleep, I should say) went smoothly. We had high hopes for the morning.

She did well that next morning, and it was determined that her respiratory failure had been from the excess fluid in her lungs. The antibiotics and anti-fungals were stopped, and she was gradually weaned off the high flow oxygen. She was fussy but seemed to improve as the day went on. In the afternoon, she was taken off high flow oxygen completely and switched back to oxygen through a nasal cannula.

She tolerated this well, but soon a new problem evolved—a high heart rate of 170s-180s. The doctors suggested that this could be a result of her now having too LITTLE fluid in her body. The Lasix which had helped remove the extra fluid that had caused her shortness of breath may have made her dehydrated (causing the high heart rate). Based on this theory, the Lasix was stopped, and by the evening her heart rate had returned to the 130s-140s.

This afternoon, however, her heart rate has crept back up to the 200s. No one has an answer as to why. She won't nurse, and her NG has been removed simply to take away one possible irritant while this mystery remains.

They put her back on high flow oxygen to see if it would lower her heart rate, but it has not helped. She will remain in the PICU until her heart rate issues are resolved.

Aunt Amy and I have the PICU watch tonight.

April 15, 2018, Sunday   5.20

Colette is eight months old today! She had a pretty good night except for general fussiness. Other than that, things looked good. Her heart rate came down to the 150s and even 140s while she slept. However, this morning, her heart rate went right back up to the 170-180s.

She's been fussy with no really good naps and no good wake periods.

They did an echocardiogram today to look at her heart because, in the attempt to discover why her blood sugar levels had been low, they found that her carnitine levels were abnormally low [an amino acid that has to do with the functioning of the heart]. *It is a random finding and no one is too concerned about it, but low carnitine levels can affect the heart, hence the echocardiogram, just to be safe. We have not gotten any results yet.*

They plan to attempt to wean her off the high flow oxygen tomorrow, if all goes well. Meanwhile, Mom and Dad have arrived, so I will head home where TJ waits for me!

April 16, 2018, Monday   5.21

Tim and I returned to the hospital today. This has been one of the most difficult times since our journey began. For so many reasons. Colette continues to show no progress and even some regression. Her rapid heart rate persists, plus her pain and agitation seems to have increased. She has not been able to come off high-flow oxygen and has instead required higher and higher levels of oxygen. Her pulse ox drops so rapidly when she cries or is lying flat. The concern is, if she continues this way, she will need to be intubated and placed on a ventilator.

The question remains: <u>Why</u>? She has had a CT scan of the abdomen, chest and sinuses which all appear normal aside from a small amount of fluid in the lungs. She's been placed back on antibiotics, had her morphine dose increased, and had an NG placed (breast milk is on hold until the risk of intubation is over though).

The medical team that is on tonight is by far the one in which I have the least confidence. There is only one person in the room that I trust—my Heavenly Father. He will orchestrate as He thinks best.

PS: I will both lay down in peace and sleep; for <u>YOU</u> alone, O Lord, make <u>Colette</u> to dwell in safety [referring to Psalm 4:8]

April 17, 2018, Tuesday   *5.22*

Praise God, Colette got through the night without needing to be intubated. This morning, however, her breathing has become very rapid. The plan for the day is to take her to the OR for a bronchoscopy which will allow for imaging of the lungs plus a sample collection. She will be brought back intubated and on a ventilator. At this point, it is a relief because her breathing has become so labored and her discomfort is so great. I just want her to get a moment's rest! They have had to increase her morphine again—still no sign of our old Colette. Lyssa came today to help hold Colette while we wait for her to be taken to the OR.

Later

The breathing tube is placed, and Colette will have a rest for "several days" according to the PICU attending doctor. The bronchoscopy went well but the images didn't show excess mucus or infection. Samples were collected and sent to the lab as planned. Perhaps they will provide answers.

Oh, how the throne of Heaven is being rushed to by God's children! I opened five or so cards today and each of them were from people I <u>know</u> are praying. Each told of their daily intercession for Colette. How will God respond?

Oh, Father, please hear us! Please touch Colette. Have mercy upon us for <u>You</u> are our hope. Healing comes from You alone so I ask <u>please</u> heal Colette and may her healing, her <u>life</u>, be a perpetual testimony of Your power and loving kindness. Like the paralyzed man who was brought by his friends to You through the roof, so <u>we</u>, the body of Christ, bring this baby to You [Luke 5:17-39]. We have faith that You can heal her, and we have faith that You will heal her according to Your character—loving, good, merciful One—<u>unless</u> a greater plan requires something else. If that be the case, I trust Your plan; not my will, but Yours be done.

91

April 18, 2018, Wednesday 5.23

Colette looks so peaceful. Such a relief to see her this way after the past several weeks. The hardest part now is not holding her! Being near her without scooping her up is torment. It's like having the most delicious dessert in the house and knowing it is not to be sampled!

At rounds the discussion circled around her kidneys. Her urine output is low and her fluid requirements (between antibiotics, blood products and nutrition) are high. She has been retaining fluids for several days which is making it harder on her lungs to recover. The renal doctors have been summoned, and a plan has been developed to start a more aggressive Lasix treatment with the hope of increasing her urine output to get rid of some of the excess fluid. This has increased her urine output, but not drastically. They will watch it overnight with the possibility of starting CRRT (continuous renal replacement therapy)[14] tomorrow if things do not improve.

Colette has also required more IV access so a double lumen PICC was placed in her right arm [an additional central line that enters through the arm and goes into the heart]. *On a positive note, they were able to start some feeds through her NG, which makes me so happy!*

While McLaine sat in the room with Colette this afternoon, Tim and I went for a walk around Wade Pond where God gave me such a gift—five loons[15] on the pond! It was glorious to see their beautiful, calm forms gliding over the water—as if to say, "In spite of the chaos of our surroundings here in the city, we have an inner peace. This world cannot fluster us for we know a secret!" Their secret, of course, is the world they are migrating back to—a world of cool, dark waters, birch trees, minnows and the Northern Lights. For them, this is just a stop in a noisy city…a stepping stone to paradise. And I, like them, can be calm in the midst of my chaos for I too know a secret—I know the God of the lakes, trees and stars. This God will help me through the darkness. Truly this is only a stepping stone to the paradise He will one day call me to.

---

[14] CRRT is a complex treatment in which a patient is connected to a machine that takes over the work of the kidneys. Blood is continuously removed from the patient and cycled through the machine which removes excess fluid and waste products and returns the remaining blood to the patient. It requires two nurses to oversee the process at all times. One nurse is responsible for monitoring the patient while the second nurse monitors the machine, making adjustments according to how the patient is responding.

[15] The common loon is a bird native to the northern parts of North America. They migrate South in the winter where they live incognito until spring when they return to their northern habitat. I grew up loving loons as they were common visitors to my family's vacationing spot in Northern Ontario. To spot loons in Ohio, let alone in the middle of a busy city in April, was extraordinarily special to me.

April 19, 2018, Thursday 5.24

Last night, Colette was so comfortable that she was able to be taken completely off one of the sedation medications. Her urine output increased to a good level; however, she is still taking in more fluids than she is losing. The nephrology and PICU team decided that CRRT should be initiated. The renal doctor emphasized to us that Colette's kidneys are working great. This measure is only being taken because her kidneys are having to work much harder than normal because of all the fluids she requires (the many antibiotics, TPN, lipids, etc.), and the excess strain is putting them at risk.

The OR team was summoned to determine where the catheter needed for the procedure could be placed, and Colette left for the OR around 11:30 AM. She returned about an hour later with an arterial line in her left wrist and a catheter for CRRT in the right side of her neck. The procedure went smoothly, and now everyone is buzzing around preparing to start CRRT. Her blood pressure did drop at one point to 50s/30s, which resulted in an epinephrine drip being added [an IV medication used to control blood pressure]*; but she has responded to this beautifully.*

I have had great peace all day. I keep telling myself: God is choosing this path for us. This is His conscious decision made out of love and wisdom. Nothing will occur by chance.

April 20, 2018, Friday 5.25

Oh, my heart has broken a million times today. Last night, her carbon dioxide levels rose drastically, which resulted in chest x-rays and a pulmonary consult that left us with nothing but questions as to why. It has since returned to a normal level. No reasons or explanations can be found. Now, however, her blood glucose levels (which up till now have only ever been abnormally low) have shot up to the 400s [normal: 70-100]. *Again there is no known reason. She has been started on an insulin drip to control her blood sugars.*

On top of this, Tim and I were told abruptly in morning rounds that there would be no round six of chemo. Dr. Stearns does not believe Colette's body could tolerate any further treatment. The focus now is to help her recover, and that is all. It should not have been a surprise to me, but I felt so horribly shocked…and so very afraid. My great dread that Colette's sixth round of chemotherapy would be canceled was set free and overwhelmed me.

As soon as rounds were over, I went inside Colette's room, pulled the curtain and cried and cried. I see now I was trusting in the chemo. I was trusting in the "plan" to cure Colette—not God. So, this news sunk me. I so badly wanted to complete the "plan." I wanted to follow all the rules, because if I did, then Colette would be healed. My faith was in the plan, in the chemo, in the protocol.

93

I took a walk with Tim and cried. I held Colette's fingers and cried. I talked to the attending doctor and cried. No other words could describe my condition better than the psalmist's "My <u>soul</u> was downcast within me" [Psalms 42:6-11].

<u>But</u> I will hope in God. I will yet praise Him! I <u>will</u> trust God—I will submit with thanksgiving to His plan, for who am I to say how things ought to be? He is my Creator— <u>He</u> is all-knowing, all-wise, all-powerful and GOOD. This plan will bring about the greatest amount of good for the greatest number of people. I can and will trust Him—I must. What do I know with my finite mind? I do not know how this will all end—but one day, I will see it for what it is…good.

No round six—Thank You Father. Thank You that this is done—no more chemo, ANC drops, months of separation as a family. Thank You for <u>Your</u> decision. I bless Your name and praise You in advance because one day I will look back and see why. One day I will see the wisdom and love behind this decision. I believe You Father—give me faith and grace to continually trust.

I left the hospital around 2:00 PM, and Colette was doing really well. Breast milk had been started through her NG; vent settings were coming down. Vital signs were stable.

Tonight, I got word from my parents that her blood pressures were dipping low (due to the fluid shifts associated with CRRT). The epinephrine drip had stabilized everything though.

In a battle now—to trust, to cast my anxiety on Him. It <u>is</u> a battle. All I <u>want</u> to do is worry, but I will not let my feelings dictate my actions.

CHAPTER 10

Days of Darkness

A pril 23, 2018, Monday   *No more counting!*
What a weekend it has been! Colette did well Friday night—just a couple of blood pressure drops. Tim returned to the hospital first thing Saturday morning to be present for rounds. Meanwhile, I woke with terrible nausea. It did not take long before the not so subtle evidence of a stomach virus convinced me that I would not be returning to Colette or enjoying any time with TJ. My parents picked up TJ on their way home from the hospital. So while I spent some quality time with the couch and the bathroom, TJ enjoyed playing "ou-side"…there is no one to match his passion for the outdoors like his Oma!

From Tim, I received updates on Colette. She had an EKG, EEG, and another echocardiogram [tests that look at heart and brain functioning] *which all looked good. Her difficulties centered around 1. Her need for a paralytic to keep her still while she remained on the ventilator (her current sedation medications weren't strong enough)[16] 2. Blood pressure drops requiring epinephrine and fluid boluses. 3. Blood glucose drops into the 40s. These problems persisted all weekend.*

---

[16] While Colette was intubated and on a ventilator, it was important that she remain still to prevent the breathing tube from dislodging (as well as to prevent her from waking up and being alarmed by her situation). The goal was to keep her calm, comfortable and still. However, it was difficult to keep her sedated enough without dropping her blood pressures and causing other negative side effects. When necessary, she would be placed on a paralytic that would essentially paralyze her muscles; however, long term use of paralytics are avoided as they have serious side effects.

I returned to the hospital on Sunday, and Colette was able to come off CRRT without any complications. She has since been able to maintain a good fluid balance (hurray!).

The battle to keep Colette sedated without a paralytic continues (she is such a wiggle worm!) as does the mystery concerning her blood sugar levels. The endocrine team is involved, but they remain as puzzled as the rest of us. She has been placed on a dextrose [sugar] infusion to combat the issue for now.

We will see what God has in store for her today!

April 24, 2018, Tuesday

What a glorious change one day has made! Tim and I woke this morning (or fully awoke from the semi-wakeful "PICU Slumber") to a flow of good news. Her daily chest x-ray looked perfect, she was taken off the paralytic, and her urine output had been steady! Because of these solid steps, big plans for the day were made and mobilized.

Her Foley and arterial line were taken out, a hearing screen was attempted (no success, however, due to electrical interference in the room?), and an MRI of the brain was scheduled for later today. They hope to extubate her tomorrow!

April 25, 2018, Wednesday

Blessed be God, all-powerful!

So many praises! She had her CRRT catheter removed [there was no longer a threat that she would require CRRT again], a lumbar puncture done by Dr. Stearns [to check the cerebral spinal fluid for any tumor cells] and she had her breathing tube removed! She did so well!

They put her on a high-flow oxygen at first, but she has since been able to move to oxygen through a regular nasal cannula! Oh, how good it felt to have her in my arms again. She spent all day (except for brief pumping sessions) in my arms.

Dr. Stearns came with the final read on the MRI: NO TUMOR! Praise God for this goodness—praise Him for raising her up again, our good and perfect gift! She is more whole than ever. I have seen miracles—I have seen the power of God. Our hope is in Him.

April 26, 2018, Thursday

Our new battle with Colette is with her withdrawal and delirium from all the medications she has had to be on. Yesterday, she was lethargic, sweaty and struggled to sleep. Around 1:00 AM she began crying in her poor hoarse, airy voice (her throat was sore from the recent intubation). She did not stop till an hour later. Then she slept fitfully until 5:30 AM when she got up for good. Since then she has had to be in either Tim or my arms. She is still very irritable.

On a positive note, her oxygen has been weaned even more (she's now getting 2 liters through the nasal cannula), and her NG feeds are being increased today with the goal of coming off TPN.

She may be transferred back to the oncology floor tomorrow!

April 30, 2018, Monday

What an eventful few days! I never seemed to have my journal when I had time to write. To continue, I went home Thursday night while Mom and Dad took over with Colette.

I returned the next morning to hear that Colette had had another difficult night of irritability and sleeplessness. I talked with the fellow about this irritability and was told that it was most likely due to delirium and withdrawal (not pain).

Colette seemed to improve as the day went on. She slept long and well in my arms and only fussed when moved or put down in the crib. Her oxygen was decreased again (1-1 1/2 liters nasal cannula), and her feeds were up to her goal. Unfortunately later in the afternoon, she began to vomit every time I laid her down for a diaper change. Eventually her feeds had to be stopped. I left for the evening when my dad arrived to give my mom backup. They were getting her prepped to be transferred back to the oncology floor.

She was transferred later in that evening and did really well the first night. On Saturday, things began to take a turn. Her inconsolability increased and her pulse ox kept dropping down into the 70s when she cried. By Saturday evening, a PACT was called, and Liz (that beloved doctor from the PICU) came and took Colette to the PICU where she was placed back on high flow oxygen. She eventually calmed and fell asleep.

She spent most of Sunday in our arms, and by the evening we were again getting smiles out of her. Today her vital signs have been stable, and though she is still on high flow oxygen, she seems more herself.

May 1, 2018, Tuesday

We made it to May! Happy glorious May Day! I remember at the beginning of this journey calculating the months out...so many months of chemo would land us...in May! "If we can just make it to May" I thought. And here we are; God has borne us through many storms and has caused us to land safely here. All praise to Him our Comforter, our Rock and our Healer.

Colette continues to make improvements, and she has even restarted physical therapy with an emphasis on tummy time (which she detests with the same passion she did in the days of yore). She is very weak. She struggles to sit up even in her Bumbo chair (or "Bimbo" chair a la Aunt Amy). Still, we are getting periodic smiles.

Her eyes, however, look so sad—very dim, but I'm sure the Dilaudid, Clonidine, Risperidone, Ativan and Benadryl take their toll [just a handful of the many medications she had to be on while she was critically ill; most of which were being weaned slowly resulting in her withdrawal irritability].

She has been taken off high flow oxygen and placed back on the oxygen through the nasal cannula. She will remain in the PICU for monitoring while she adjusts to this change. Hopefully she will do just fine!

May 2, 2018, Wednesday

Overnight, Colette's pulse ox continually dropped resulting in her being placed back on high flow oxygen. Because of her drops in oxygen saturation, her NG feeds have been stopped, and TPN has been restarted. The doctors do not know why her lungs are still struggling to maintain proper oxygenation. They started her on a round of steroids to see if it helps.

May 5, 2018, Friday

Yesterday morning I thought I knew what it was to fear. But all I knew yesterday morning was a low grade fear—a fear that far off in the distance there is a threat that may or may not be coming. Yesterday evening I came to know true fear and her children: terror and despair; but thank God, they have gone for now.

Tim and I arrived yesterday morning in time for rounds. The mystery remained as to why she had the periods of low oxygenation the day before, but the doctors were pleased with how she looked and began the process of weaning her off the high flow oxygen.

During rounds, the resident doctor mentioned in a very casual way that Colette had an elevated BNP of >5000 and requested a consult with cardiology [BNP is a hormone that is affected by the heart. Normal levels are less than 125]. *The first cardiologists that came to examine Colette assured us that the BNP number isn't very important for children, etc. and that we should not be too concerned. We promptly ignored this new threat and gloried in the fact that Colette was doing so well—smiling, doing PT and weaning off high flow oxygen.*

When the next cardiologist [a more senior member of the cardiology team] *came to examine Colette, she did not share her colleague's carefree attitude. She noted that Colette's liver was enlarged. She then ordered an echocardiogram which confirmed her suspicion that the right side of Colette's heart was enlarged (which had caused the elevated BNP). She also told us that there was a hole in Colette's heart that had not closed properly when she had been born (PFO). This hole is common in children and typically benign. However, in Colette it had posed a problem because it allowed blood to move from the left to the right side of the heart (opposite of the way it should flow) resulting in non-oxygenated blood being sent to her body. This is what had led to her mysterious periods of low oxygen saturations. The backward flow of blood increased when Colette cried, which explains why she had always had low pulse ox readings when crying. This enlargement of the right side of the heart and the backward flow of blood all resulted from increased pressure in the blood vessels of the lungs, a condition called pulmonary hypertension.*

Now the question becomes, why was there increased pressure in the blood vessels of the lungs [pulmonary hypertension]*? The two most probable causes are pulmonary embolisms* [clots in the blood vessels of the lungs] *or a very rare complication from chemo called VOD (veno-occlusive disorder).*

The doctors first wanted to check for clots in the lungs. To do this they would need to intubate her and do a CT scan of her chest. Tim and I were sent out of the room while they prepared to intubate Colette. Tim went for a walk while I waited in the Serenity Room.

Minutes later, the attending doctor came to get me saying, "Colette has started seizing, if you want to come with me..."

It was like that moment when we were first told about the "mass." A very "out of body experience." I felt faint and numb with terror. I mechanically followed the doctor to the room. As I entered, I saw her lying on the bed still seizing on her right side. The medical team was busily working all around her, medicating her to stop the seizure and preparing her to be taken for the CT scan. The CT scan would now look, not only for clots in her lungs, but also for the cause of the seizure. I was told the seizure could be caused by 1. a brain bleed 2. the tumor's return 3. a stroke

In that moment it feels like the inside of you dies—like you are a shell that can move and talk, but the real you inside is dead.

Tim soon returned to the room, and when Colette had stopped seizing we followed the medical team that was wheeling her little bed down to the radiology department. Over and over I repeated the verse that came to my mind, "And the Lord, He is the One who goes before you. He will be with you, He will not leave you nor forsake you; do not fear nor be dismayed." [Deut. 31:8]

Tim and I stood outside the room while they scanned her, and we regrouped. We told ourselves: God sovereignly has chosen this for us. He is in control. He is good. One day we will understand God's reasons for this nightmare. We can praise Him in advance for what seems to make no sense in the present.

On the way back she was horribly pale. I was terrified. Was she hemorrhaging as we walked? The team raced her back to the room. Doctors and nurses surrounded her bed and worked quickly; Tim and I silently watched. An arterial line was placed, and she was connected to an EEG which would monitor for any further seizure activity. Before long the CT results were read. They showed no strokes, bleeds or tumors. I cannot write this without saying THANK YOU GOD! Gradually, her color returned to her face, and we were told that she was out of immediate danger. Shaking with relief, Tim and I thanked God for sparing our little girl.

She did well through the night. The EEG reading had shown no further signs of seizures, and the focus this morning has been on preparing Colette for an MRI. This will provide a more detailed look at her brain, and perhaps find the cause of her seizure.

She has been placed on nitric oxide (INO) which is an inhaled medication that causes the blood vessels in the lungs to dilate, thereby decreasing pulmonary hypertension. Her BNP levels are coming down which indicate that the INO is helping.

The two questions remain: what caused the pulmonary hypertension that led to the right side of her heart being enlarged and what caused the seizure?

Later

Colette left for the MRI around 11:30 this morning and returned around 2:00 this afternoon. The MRI showed that Colette has several small clots in her brain, which presumably led to her seizure. The clots, we have been assured, are very small. These findings, however, have led the team to believe that the pulmonary hypertension is due to small clots in the lungs as well. Heparin has been ordered to reduce the risk of new clots forming. She remains intubated and on a ventilator. For now, she is calm.

What would I do if I thought I was in the hands of fate? But chance or fate has not one finger in this. Everything has been purposefully prescribed by my good Father. I trust You Lord. Give me grace to bear this ache.

May 6, 2018, Sunday

Yesterday Colette's BNP continued its downward trend. There was so much improvement that the doctors decided to attempt to take her off the ventilator today. She was successfully extubated at 11:30 AM. She's been an angel since—she even took a mouth swab full of breast milk! It is wonderful holding her again.

May 7, 2018, Monday

Oh, Colette, you are a darling!

She did all right last night; she was up about every two hours. She won't nurse, but did take another mouth swab full of breast milk. She continues on the high flow oxygen and the INO. The cardiologists have ordered another echocardiogram to be done today which will show how the pulmonary hypertension and heart enlargement is progressing.

May 8, 2018, Tuesday

I'm writing from Angie's Garden, the rooftop garden here at Rainbow. I've stepped away from Colette's room for a bit to get some fresh air, and oh, the sunshine! Colette continues to improve. She is up to full feeds through her NG, and her oxygen needs have decreased. The doctors hope that if she continues doing this well, she will be able to come off the high flow oxygen and be put on oxygen through a nasal cannula. They also want to determine if she can come off the INO. Unfortunately, she is not able to leave the PICU until this is achieved.

Physical therapy and occupational therapy have resumed and are going well. Colette still refuses to nurse but will take sponges full of milk occasionally.

As for the echocardiogram results, they showed that the right side of her heart has returned to a normal size! The pressure inside the heart has normalized, and the backwards flow of blood has ceased. Praise God, what an answer to prayer!

It is so beautiful out. Stephanie (the child life specialist) and I are planning to get Colette up here to the garden as soon as possible. Sunshine for Coco!

May 9, 2018, Wednesday

Hurray for Colette—God continues to work! I can't help but smile at daily rounds—five attending doctors gathered this morning (cardiology, pulmonology, ICU, hemoncology and palliative) to discuss Colette's case, and they are all stumped. No one understands what happened or why it happened. Theories float back and forth and seem to vary with whoever is walking through the door. They all agree, however, that she is getting better. I smile, not only because she is improving but also because of God. He alone knows what He is doing and why. We, with all our most brilliant minds on it, can merely speculate.

Praise God for His might! He casts down, and He raises up again according to His own wise, good counsel.

Colette continues to tolerate her NG feeds, and she is off the high flow oxygen and on oxygen through the nasal cannula. They are attempting to wean the INO today (an all-day process). Meanwhile, Colette is growing more active!

Going home with Tim to be with TJ tonight; Poppa and Oma have a date with Miss Colette.

May 11, 2018, Friday

Yesterday was simply glorious. Through a donated gift to the oncology floor, I was able to go to John Robert's Spa for Mother's Day. Three other mothers from the oncology floor were there as well, and we spent the whole morning together. It was simply heavenly. It was so nice to talk with these other moms—to not feel as though I'm in a room full of people who don't understand. These women all <u>did</u> understand. They all had their own 3:00 AM terrors. They all knew the reluctance to gaze into the future. They all had thoughts that they refused to think, let alone speak aloud.

Afterwards I returned to the hospital where Colette was completely off INO. She was slightly more agitated but still doing very well.

Mom and I stayed the night with her, and today she seems even more out of sorts.

Later

Colette had an echocardiogram that showed a return of the increased pressure in the right side of her heart. It is not as bad as before, but enough to require treatment again with the INO. It has been restarted along with a medication called Sildenafil. It is an oral medication that the doctors hope will be able to replace the inhaled INO once it reaches a therapeutic level in her system. When this is achieved, the INO will once more be stopped, and we will see how her heart and lungs respond. We cannot leave the PICU until she is off the INO.

May 12, 2018, Saturday

Colette certainly made some progress today with regard to her irritability. We even had some periods of smiling and serious feet kicking! I also did a little tummy time with her (which she detested with vigor).

She has gotten a little congested which is a side effect of Sildenafil, but she doesn't seem too bothered by it.

Hoping to see continued improvements tomorrow!

May 13, 2018, Sunday   *Mother's Day*

What a broken-hearted Mother's Day. It has been seven weeks since Colette was admitted to the hospital.

She woke at 5:00 AM completely congested and agitated. From that point on, she became a poor, miserable fixture in my arms. Her cries could not be more pitiful. They are so soft and seem despairing. I am told that the congestion is due to the Sildenafil, and no medication can counteract it. She needs the Sildenafil to get off the INO. She needs to get off the INO so we can get out of the PICU. There is nothing that can be done to help her. Poor, poor girl...

I left later in the morning to go see TJ while Tim stayed with Colette until my parent's arrival. I cried the entire way home.

However, TJ's sheer bliss at my arrival temporarily lifted my spirits. We had a fantastic morning together. But when I put him down for a nap, Tim called to give me an update saying that Colette's congestion and agitation had gotten worse. What is so hard to bear is that no one knows why this is going on or how to resolve it.

I am so very low. Is this to be our life? Making a little progress then falling deeper, a cycle from which there is no ultimate victory? Every time Colette starts to improve, I feverishly begin building castles in the air only to have them ripped down just as I reach their completion.

Tim left Colette in my parent's care. I am waiting for him to get home now, so I can go to the hospital if she doesn't improve. I just beg God for a miracle. Heal her, Father! Have mercy on us and heal her...

May 14, 2018, Monday

Colette has improved. After I finished writing yesterday, I melted to the floor. I was so exhausted and so desperate for God to intervene. I cried out to Him, and He met my sorrow with compassion. Within minutes my mom called me. She said that a respiratory therapist had come to the room and decided to try deep suctioning to see if it would relieve the congestion...and it worked! Praise God it worked! I soon was getting videos of a transformed Colette, full of smiles and kicking her little feet. I cannot describe my joy and my thankfulness. Praise God Who hears and answers prayers!

Per mom's report today, Colette continues to be happy and content. The pulmonary team examined the echocardiograms that were done on Friday and Saturday and said that there were slight improvements. They want to do a VQ scan and a CT [imaging done to look at the blood vessels of the lungs] *tomorrow just to make sure they are not missing anything contributing to her pulmonary hypertension.* [They were still unsure what had caused the pulmonary hypertension in the first place; without knowing the exact cause, it was difficult to know how to prevent it from happening again.]

Meanwhile, I just keep praying to our miracle-working Great Physician.

May 15, 2018, Tuesday

Happy nine months, Colette! Tim, TJ and I went to the hospital first thing this morning. On our arrival, the room was empty as Colette was down in the Nuclear Medicine Department with my mom getting her VQ scan. TJ and I impatiently set off to find her, and when we succeeded TJ was able to see Colette for the first time since Easter! He was so excited even though "Coco sleeping?" Yes TJ, a lovely Ketamine-induced nap! [She was under sedation at the time to keep her still for the VQ scan].

When Colette was taken back to her room, TJ was then able to interact with her a little before going home with Oma. Tim and I stayed with Colette who seemed very happy and content. The results of the VQ scan looked perfect. The entire team will meet tomorrow to pool all the information we have so far and develop a plan for the near future.

For the present, the plan is to slowly increase her Sildenafil dose until it reaches the full therapeutic dose in her system (some time this weekend), and then she will be weaned off the INO and high flow oxygen. We have to remain in the PICU until this can be achieved. Slow progress…slow progress.

May 16, 2018, Wednesday

Today has been a busy day—I've begun writing this several times but just kept getting interrupted! We started the morning with a 6:00 AM vomit after which Colette refused to go back to sleep. She was full of energy and smiles until her first morning nap.

At rounds it was decided that Colette would have a pretty calm day, the only change being a tiny increase in her Sildenafil dose. After rounds I left Tim at the hospital with Colette to meet Lyssa at Toys R US/Babies R Us for their going-out-of-business sale. I got Colette her new big girl car seat plus several other items (including a Water Baby! I couldn't resist…it was one of my childhood favorites!) After making my purchases, I buzzed back to the hospital to find that Colette had vomited two more times plus had had several episodes of diarrhea. The NG feeds were stopped, and GI was being consulted.

Meanwhile, the promised team meeting led by Dr. Stearns involving hemoncology, pulmonology, ICU, and palliative had begun. They determined that the number one goal was to get Colette to a full dose of Sildenafil while slowly weaning her off INO (hopefully she will be completely off by tomorrow afternoon).

After this is achieved, she will have an echocardiogram to see how her heart is responding. God-willing, it will be normal. If not, she will be given more time on the INO, and a heart catheterization and lung biopsy will be done to search for more answers. The tests they have done up to this point have been inconclusive. They do not know why she developed pulmonary hypertension, but they hope, whatever the original cause, she will make a full recovery.

The GI department made several suggestions regarding her vomiting; however, Dr. Stearns holds to the opinion that a sensitive stomach is simply part of Colette for the time being. He says that since it is not affecting her growth, we should not be overly concerned. At this point, I agree.

May 17, 2018, Thursday

Progress continues to be made—Colette is off INO! She has not had any more vomiting or diarrhea and is at a therapeutic dose of Sildenafil.

We're waiting for her echocardiogram results to see how her heart is responding, but so far, her vital signs look great…heart rate is nice and low.

She has had two great days with regard to energy—she stayed up last night until 10:00 PM! Her little "merry legs" kept kicking with joy!

May 18, 2018, Friday

Today Colette saw…SUNLIGHT! We took her up to Angie's rooftop garden this afternoon! Not being tethered down by INO or high flow oxygen any longer, the natural thing to do on a beautiful May day would be to soar upward. Am I right? That is exactly what we did!

It was a cheerful little parade—Tim, the nurse, our resident friend Allison and I accompanied Colette who was dressed in a rainbow of colors and styling pink star sunglasses. Her happy little feet were kicking overtime!

It's very much like waking up from a nightmare. All of a sudden, it is over. The fear and the terror of the last eight weeks and the dread of the one thing I would not let myself think is OVER. She is back.

Oh, praise the name of the Lord Who raises up—bless Him forever and ever! He has heard our prayers! He has reached down to earth, and by His mighty arm, He has restored our girl. I can never again say I have not seen a miracle for Colette herself is a miracle.

And to wake up from a nightmare to this…to spring! The past seven months there were no seasons—it was a year in which the calendar turned, but we paid it no mind. We *lived by rounds, not months. But I am awake. The nightmare is vanishing. The whole world and my whole life seems reborn.*

I remember several months ago writing at my kitchen table looking out into my snow-filled backyard and feeling that it reflected my life. I sit now at the same spot. I look out into my yard filled now with evening sun. TJ's swing and the bird feeders are swaying just slightly in the breeze, and it is beautiful. It is ready to welcome home the two children that will bring with them <u>life</u>. Joy is coming.

PS: I am so thankful for the nightmare…it has been a gift from God. It has transformed me, and I would not want to erase it from my life even if I could. Spring is more glorious because of the darkness of winter.

May 19, 2018, Saturday

Another wonderful day. Colette continues to do well. So well that she has returned to the oncology floor! Farewell PICU! After six weeks in intensive care, she is taking steps towards home.

Meanwhile, TJ and I had a marvelous day at home. We spent the morning working on the yard. We weeded, planted and shaped the gardens; TJ loved it all! He is all about the watering can and shovel. When the rain hit, we enjoyed time inside playing with his stuffed animals, play dough and cars, cars, cars! These are beautiful days.

May 21, 2018, Monday

Tim and I returned to Colette last evening as TJ went to Poppa and Oma's. Colette is doing well, but what troubles me today is that her heart rate is a little higher than normal. She is also a bit more irritable than she has been for a while. The pulmonary hypertension team came to check on her and ordered an echocardiogram for tomorrow just to check. I'm praying for another miracle.

They attempted to wean her completely off oxygen today, but she just wasn't able to do it. Every time they decreased the oxygen to ¼ liter she would drop her oxygen saturations.

I'm praying for contentment.

May 22, 2018, Tuesday

Her echocardiogram today showed no changes from Friday, which is wonderful—whatever caused her increased heart rate and irritability is not pulmonary hypertension.

Thank You, God!

Baby steps forward now seems to be our motto—Colette is now down to 1/8th liter of oxygen! It is amazing how truly she needs that 1/8th liter! She cannot hold her saturation levels up without it! She has also been started on a very slow wean from all her pain/anti-nausea medications. Every day one of the medications is weaned a tiny bit as a part of a month long wean protocol.

Otherwise, she spent most of the day snoozing in my arms.

May 23, 2018, Wednesday
Colette's appearance changes every day as her eyebrows come in and her eyelashes get more delicious! She is so beautiful.

Today she had a make-up sleep day as she was up quite a bit last night! She still needs her 1/8th liter of oxygen, but the medication wean continues to go well.

The big event of the day was blood in her last three diapers. Her lab work came back fine, indicating that the blood loss is not substantial. Still, the cause is a mystery. They are holding her daily Lovenox shot [a medication used to prevent blood clots; it has the potential to cause bleeding]. *I'm just praying that whatever the cause God will heal it as well.*

As for TJ, I was able to FaceTime with him! He appears to be having the time of his life at Poppa and Oma's. So all is well for him.

May 27, 2018, Sunday
The days have slipped by—many horrible and glorious ones all jumbled together. But all in all, Colette continues to improve. The blood in her diapers has stopped which, though unexplained, is wonderful news. The pinnacle of joy occurred yesterday when Colette came off oxygen COMPLETELY! Miracles of miracles! What progress she has made!

May 28, 2018, Monday   *Memorial Day*
What a memorable Memorial Day! Colette and I got up for the day around 7:30 AM. We had a lovely morning together. I worked on bottle feeding with her (not very successfully I might add), and she had a snuggle nap (which involves her napping while I snuggle her). She is so beautiful while she naps. I just hold her and drink in her down-right

adorableness. Her eyelashes are getting so long and are making her big, mesmerizing eyes even more dramatic. Her eyebrows have returned as dark as ever, and her hair gets longer every day.

Tim and TJ came around 11:00 AM, and the day got even sweeter. We took both children to the playroom where TJ played and Colette watched. We were our own Memorial Day parade traveling up and down the hall. TJ led our company, proudly holding Colette's foot, while I carried Colette and Tim followed with the IV pole (or "Poleen" as we lovingly refer to the IV pole).

Afterwards, we all went to Angie's Garden where we basked in the sunshine, played with bubbles and got some cute star-shaped sunglasses.

After our time in the sun, we enjoyed some lunch. Then Tim and TJ left for Grammy and Grampy's. Colette napped for a while then got up for more occupational and physical therapy…and singing and books and fun.

Colette and I spent the evening together. After such a sweet day, I began feeling surprisingly low at its finish. But God is here with us girls. It is good to be alone—to be silent and feel His presence.

May 29, 2018, Tuesday
Colette did beautifully last night. Her wean off her medications continues to go well—it is a very slow process, but I am trying to avoid the urge to rush things. Mom and Kayla are coming to visit today; then Tim and TJ will join us this evening.

It has been decided that since Colette continues to refuse to take any food or fluids by mouth (in spite of all the work occupational therapy has done with her) a G-tube[17] will be surgically placed in order to do away with the NG for good. They may have an opening in the OR tomorrow.

---

[17] A G-tube is a small tube that goes through the skin of the abdomen into the stomach. An extension tube can be attached which allows liquified food, fluids and medicines to go directly into the stomach through a pump or a syringe. It was a wonderful step for us because feeds through the NG had become increasingly difficult, especially as Colette had become more curious about the NG tube that always hung so temptingly down the side of her face!

May 30, 2018, Wednesday

Surgery day! Colette is having the G-tube placed right now. We will see how she does post-operatively, but they are preparing us that she may need to go to the PICU for observation if she has difficulty with her breathing.

May 31, 2018, Thursday

The surgery went beautifully, and we are back on Mac 6—no PICU for us! She got the G-tube, and although there was a little concern about her breathing afterwards, she managed perfectly on 2 liters of oxygen.

During rounds this morning, the magical word was spoken…HOME! Dr. Stearns wants us home on Monday! Oh, how thrilling that sounds. I can't believe it!

Before then, we have to take a G-tube care class, get all the medications she needs, and make follow-up appointments (Dr. Stearns/OT/PT/Speech). Colette has to get to full feeds through her G-tube, get off Ativan, Benadryl and Zofran [nausea medications], try a window without food to see how her blood sugar levels hold, have an echocardiogram and STAY OUT OF TROUBLE!

At home…we need to clean!

June 1, 2018, Friday

Welcome June! Oh, what high hopes I have for you!
Colette had a fussy night but is doing great this morning. Today she comes off Zofran and Ativan; plus they are doing a four hour window of no feeds to see if she can maintain her blood sugar levels.

June 3, 2018, Sunday

Colette continues to make progress—so much so that we anticipate that she will go home tomorrow! It is ten weeks today since she left home…seven months since this journey began. Strangely, I feel overwhelmed with what is about to happen—terrified to shut the pages of this chapter in our lives. As horrible and painful as they were, they were still so precious—so filled with Colette. What will the next chapter hold? There is such an underlying fear—a nagging, thieving fear that refuses to let me rejoice with the others. A fear so terrifying that I cannot even write it. But I have learned in these past seven months, and here I go. I will take my mind and walk it through the paths of truth until it reaches the Rock that is higher than I.

God is Sovereign: He writes the script of my life. He alone dictates the next step. Chance doesn't have a say in what comes our way.

God is Good: His sovereign plan will be filtered through His infinite goodness. One day, I will look back and praise Him for every choice He made for me because I will see that It was good. If it is painful now, it means that the story is not over. I must keep going.

God is wise: He knows what the next step should be. If it doesn't appear to make sense, it is because His mind is infinite and mine is finite.
God is faithful. Never, ever, ever will I be alone. He will ever be at my side. The God of all-comfort, imminent, and omnipresent is loyal to me.

God's grace will always be enough. He will never let it be too much for me. <u>Do Not Fear The Future.</u>

Praise God—What an amazing good, good God. Bless His name forever—it is by Him alone we stand.

Praise Him.

CHAPTER 11

There Is No Place Like Home

J*une 5, 2018, Tuesday*   *HOME!*

We are home! Oh, how good it feels to all be here together. I keep thinking of that passage in Ecclesiastes that talks about there being a season for everything—this is our "season to build" [Ecclesiastes 3:1-8]. Our season to build a family that is whole, strong, unified and beautiful. Yet I know, unless the Lord builds our home we labor in vain [Psalm 127:1]. So I pray, God, please build our home. Make it centered on You. Be our Cornerstone; be our King. Teach us our roles and give us grace to fulfill them.

As for yesterday…

Colette had her echocardiogram first thing in the morning which showed that the pressure in her heart has improved since last time! Dr. Stearns will try taking her off Sildenafil in a month to see how she tolerates it. After we received the echocardiogram results, Tim and I ran around filling prescriptions and packing. By three in the afternoon all of Colette's well-wishers had arrived: Jenn, Hannah (PICU nurses), Allison, Noopur and Priscilla (resident doctors…Priscilla was the resident who first told us that Colette had "a mass" on that horrible, horrible night), the nurses from the oncology floor and many of our family members. Around 4:00, Colette was carried down the hallway to the "End of

Treatment Bell" where TJ and Colette rang out our joy as a symbol of completion of chemotherapy. There were tears and smiles as we left our fellow warriors behind and went home.

It is amazing being home. We have both our darlings within reach! Tim and I keep looking at each other and smiling. Hurray! Hurray! Hurray!

Picture: Colette back in her own room...there's no place like home!

June certainly became a month of building—building routines, structure as well as new and glorious memories. God, in His wise providence, arranged this first month home during a perfect time of year. Tim was off work as his school had let out for the summer, and we took full advantage of this time together, spending most of our days outdoors.

During this time, Colette's feeding difficulties continued to plague us. Colette would not take any liquid or food by mouth, so her entire nutritional needs were met through formula and water that was mixed and delivered by a pump through her new G-tube. Her feeds during the day would typically run over an hour and were given every three hours. At first this task was complicated by our ignorance. We had been sent home with an IV pole to which the pump attached. This pump and IV pole became her jolly side-kick a third of the day, and one can only imagine how adept we become at carrying Colette and the IV pole up and down the stairs! We mastered the art of finding the particular angle that the pole had to be carried in order to prevent the top from scraping the ceiling and the bag of formula from falling off. It was a skill that came only with repetition, and we had the privilege of quite a bit of repetition. We became so talented, and the days became so beautiful, that we refused to let the pole keep us indoors! Out we went, Colette, TJ, Tim, the pole and I for walks!

All was going well with the arrangement until one day at an outpatient clinic visit I began talking with the dietician about the pole situation and inquired how parents of toddlers managed it. She then made the breakthrough announcement that the tiny backpack that had accompanied the IV pole on our discharge was a portable option for carrying the pump. Imagine our shock! A quick instructional video on how to set up the portable pump inside the backpack and our lives were never the same. Now there was no stopping us—Colette joined us on bike rides and trips to the park while the poor little IV pole was left behind, dedicated for naps and nighttime duties.

Solving the logistics of Colette's feeds came much easier than solving her tolerance for those feeds. She continued to vomit multiple times a day, and we worked with Dr. Stearns, the dietician, and a GI doctor to develop plans for improvement. My journal entries record various heroic efforts to ease her troubles: less feeds during the day with more at night, stopping and starting feeds during the night, no feeds at all through the night. No matter how creative we got, Colette continued to vomit, I continued to change linens, and the medical team continued to shrug! It did not affect her growth, and for the most part did not upset her, so we simply accepted it as part of our new life.

Because of all the medical monitoring that Colette required, Rainbow Hospital continued to play a major role in our lives. Colette had an outpatient clinic visit with Dr. Stearns once a week where her lab work was obtained and her weight was monitored. A neurologist began to play a larger role in Colette's care during this time as well. She told us that Colette was doing remarkably well. She showed no difference between the right and left side of her body. We were told that this was "unbelievable" considering her medical history. Colette would continue to require prophylactic seizure medication; however, the neurologist assured us that she did not expect any future seizures.

Overall we were encouraged by our weekly outpatient clinic visits. Dr. Stearns scheduled an MRI for the middle of July in order to check for any tumor regrowth, but by all outward signs Colette was thriving as was our family. We began to dream again—to lift our eyes from the present and gaze at the future with hope. I would listen to Dr. Stearns and the neurologist during Colette's appointments and hear phrases like "we don't know how the chemo she has received will affect her when she begins going to school, etc.," and I would hear only "going to school..." and would relish those words. Tiny buds of hope sprang up in my heart: Colette may get well. Colette may never have cancer again. Colette may grow up. Colette may one day go to school. I did not yet dare believe those dreams for the fear of the great evil returning was still too real, too present; but hope is a difficult thing to stifle—especially in the heart of an optimist.

Aside from doctor appointments, Colette was also going to Rainbow for her therapy. She required both occupational and physical therapy. Occupational therapy focused primarily on getting Colette to eat and drink by mouth. She was doing neither at this point. It was not that she COULD not; it was that she WOULD not. We were told that her oral aversion stemmed from the various unpleasant oral sensations that had played so heavily a role in her past (vomiting, intubations, NG tubes, etc.). This aversion was not confined to only edible items, but extended to anything touching her face. She would not let any item near her face—no toys, no wash clothes and certainly no bottles or spoons. She would use all skill and power to avoid them, and if all else failed she would melt into tears. I took Colette to her occupational therapy sessions at Rainbow weekly, which inevitably turned into sessions of tears. Every gallant attempt to overcome Colette's barriers was met with heartbreak. Her physical therapy sessions were little different. Colette was ten months old at this point and was not yet sitting on her own. The therapist worked with Colette to build muscle strength and coordination. Wailing and crying were a part of every session, and the unavoidable vomit was the sad finale.

However, there was one person who slipped passed Colette's well-guarded defenses and became first her friend, and eventually the one who opened the door to Colette's eating (though it would not be for a long time yet). Mary was the occupational therapist who came to us through Help Me Grow. She had the gentleness, and above all, the patience to work with Colette in a way that eventually won Colette's heart. Sessions with Mary were done weekly in our home, and tears played no part in them. Mary was a joy to us all and would remain so in the months to come.

And so these days in June were filled with learning, growth, building, and above, all joy. This leads to the final entry of the journal I had started months earlier:

June 21, 2018, Thursday

Happy first day of summer! Oh, how our God has been good to us! He has valiantly carried us through Colette's first fall, winter and spring and has brought us into a season of summer—of celebration and joy. Blessed be our God Who has gotten us the victory! Oh, it is good to be one of His children. It is bliss to rest in the sovereign, wise, good hands of such a Father. I look back to the opening entry of this journal, and I skim through the entries between—what a story this book contains! It certainly does contain her story, a story of incredible strength and resilience. It also contains our story—an amazing tale of team work and of bearing one another's burdens. Most reassuring to me, however, is that it contains His story—the story our faithful Father has written for us. It is one that has not come to its end; however, knowing my Father, I trust that the end will be one of beauty, glory and sweetness. For I know He makes all things beautiful in His time [Ecc. 3:11]. So as I close this journal, I close knowing it is but the end of one season and the beginning of another. Regardless of what this new season brings, I know the end, the REAL end of the story, will be glorious.

We entered July on that wave of thankful joy. As the Fourth of July approached, we began making plans for Colette's first holiday at home.

CHAPTER 12

The Shattering of Perfection

y journal entry on July 1st records plans for the pool and even plans for dinner—but no plan, or any insight into what was about to oc-cur. The following entry was written on what I had anticipated would be Colette's first holiday at home.

July 4, 2018, Wednesday   *Independence Day*

Colette seems to enjoy spending her holidays with her friends at Rainbow. On Monday Colette had been fussier than normal and needed some Tylenol. We assumed it was her teeth that were bothering her and thought nothing of it. At 4:30 PM she felt warm to the touch, so I took her temperature. It was 100.3 F, not quite a fever, but I called the on-call oncology fellow anyway. I was told to bring Colette to the ER for an evaluation (I later learned that he thought I had said 103 not 100.3…a mistake God clearly had orches-trated for Colette's good).

Tim stayed with TJ while I took Colette to the hospital. I was not overly concerned because she had no other signs of anything wrong other than a slight fever and fussiness. She was drooling quite a bit which also added to the hypothesis that her teeth were the culprit.

In the ER Colette was playful and happy. They took her labs and collected blood cultures along with a urine sample. Because she was doing so well and her preliminary labs

117

came back looking good, we were allowed to go home around 9:00 PM. The ER doctor told me that they would call us with her blood culture results the next day.

She slept well that night, but our morning routine was interrupted by a phone call from the ER. Colette's blood cultures came back showing a blood stream infection. They told us to take Colette to the outpatient clinic where she would be given IV antibiotics and eventually admitted to the oncology floor for further treatment.

This resulted in a rapid shift in our day. Tim and I quickly packed Colette's things, and I set off once more for the hospital. On our arrival more labs were drawn and an antibiotic was started. Colette was sleeping during this but woke just as the infusion stopped and began scream crying, tremoring and vomiting. It was horrifying. I quickly called the nurse, stripped her soiled clothes off and wrapped her in a warm blanket, holding her until the doctors came. It was, as I learned later, a "cytokine storm" a systemic response of the body resulting from the death of the particular kind of bacteria that had caused her blood stream infection. She spiked a fever of 103.8 F, and her blood pressure dropped. Eventually, she calmed back down and slept in my arms while she received an IV fluid bolus for the low blood pressure. When she woke, she was calm but her smiles were gone. I rocked her while we waited for her room on the oncology floor to be ready.

Eventually Tim came and helped us set up our Mac 6006 home. Colette perked up with Motrin and Tylenol and became more her cheerful self.

I left that evening to be with TJ while Tim remained with Colette. She apparently had another "storm" during the next antibiotic dose. Tim called me during it, and I desperately called everyone I knew that lived nearby to find someone to stay with TJ so I could get back to the hospital. Eventually a kind neighbor ran down and sat at the house (TJ was already asleep for the night), and I made my way. When I arrived, Tim was holding Colette, and they were both covered with diarrhea and vomit (thankfully not Tim's!). We worked together to get Colette clean and snug; she was sound asleep by midnight!

In the morning Tim left to spend the day with TJ while Oma (who, through God's wise providence, made a last-minute decision to remain home from a trip out of the country!) came to the hospital to celebrate the holiday with Colette and I. Colette did well all day. The bacteria causing the infection was identified, and the antibiotics were adjusted accordingly. They believe the source of the infection was her Broviac, so on the Fourth of July Colette was taken to the OR to have her Broviac removed with the hopes that it would speed up her recovery. That night, the fireworks were going off in true Cleveland form, but with our white noise to the rescue, we slept soundly in Mac 6006.

Today Colette continues to improve. She no longer has fevers, and she had an echo-cardiogram today which showed that she no longer has pulmonary hypertension! What a miracle—praise God! The plan now is for her to be on antibiotics for ten days following her first negative blood culture (which we hope will be today). They want to place a PICC line [a temporary central line that enters through the arm and goes into the heart] *on Monday, which will allow her to receive her IV antibiotics at home. Dr. Stearns has also scheduled her brain MRI. Since she is already inpatient, he decided to push up her routine scan a couple weeks so we won't have to make a special trip to the hospital for it later this month.*

Meanwhile, Colette and I have spent a gloriously uneventful day together; I have high hopes for a good night!

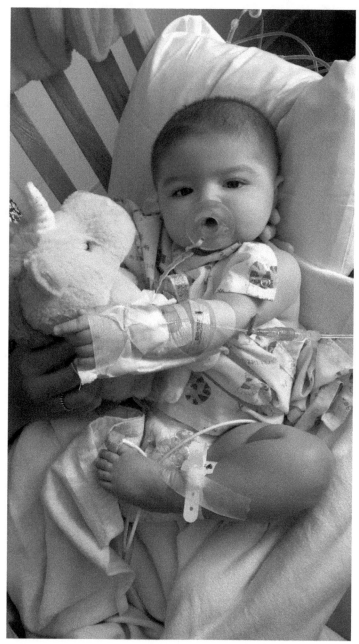

Picture: Back in the land of lines and tubing…but always surrounded by love

July 6, 2018, Friday

Colette had a good night—I ended up letting her sleep in her stroller (which was extremely convenient as I was able to give her a few pushes when she woke up, and she soon rocked back to sleep!). She had a cruel wake up call at 6:50 AM by a phlebotomist needing to draw her blood…lights on, Colette woken and moved into the bed, needle poke—not fun!

Then I got the surprising announcement that her MRI would be today instead of Monday! Tim came to the hospital to join us, and Mom took charge of TJ. The MRI went smoothly; now we just wait for results.

Later

My God is only ever good—He is sovereign, He is good. Though I do not understand, though I feel my insides crumbling, He has decided that Colette's tumor must return. He would not willingly hurt us like this, so I must believe that there is some great good that will be accomplished through this that could come no other way.

His own Son Jesus suffered for the good of many—why should I complain if my daughter has been chosen for a similar fate?

Dr. Stearns said that the regrowth is about 2 mm—the size of a grain of rice. All I can think of is what Christ said we could do if we have faith the size of a mustard seed [Matt. 17:20].

Lord, I believe You can heal her; yet I do not assume to know if You <u>should</u>. So Father, I ask You please find a way to accomplish more good by healing her than by her death. But not as I will, let Your will be done.

July 7, 2018, Saturday

My beautiful fairy-land life seems to have crumbled to pieces again. It hurts so badly. I flip-flop between trying to rationalize and force on rose-colored glasses and despairing with disgust because the poor glasses are shattered. It hurts to be with her; it hurts to be away from her. My whole heart is full of love, and the more I love her the more pain I feel. The advice I keep getting is to take things "one day at a time…one moment at a time…one second at a time etc." I must, for any more would be unbearable.

God help me.

July 8, 2018, Sunday

    I read Psalms 115 last night. God's glory is to go to no one but Him—what a set up for a miracle we are in. What potential for God's name to be praised. Tim and I are praying that God will remove Colette's tumor before the brain/spine MRI that Dr. Stearns ordered to be done in the next couple of days. It would be nothing for Him to do it—so simple! And every eye would see the power of our God. We ask as children—not knowing the implications of what we ask. Still, we ask. And we wait for our Father's wise, good decision.

July 9, 2018, Monday

    Colette continues to do so well. She had her lumbar puncture and PICC placed today. Both procedures went smoothly, praise God. She recovered so well that we were able to take her up to Angie's Garden afterwards.

    I am a little ruffled in spirit tonight because Dr. Stearns decided not to do another brain MRI just another spine MRI. I so wanted another brain MRI—I wanted to see God do a miracle and remove the tumor before man raised a finger to do anything. I want her to be fully healed, but I wanted God to get the glory alone. Or is it that I just want her healed now, and I don't want to wait. I don't know…maybe both. I'm just going to rest on my sovereign Father's wise, goodness tonight because I don't know what is next.

July 10, 2018, Tuesday

    There is such a disconnect between the Colette I see and hold and the conversations we are having with the doctors. Colette is all smiles and jabbers—how she loves her feet! She grabs one foot in each hand and just kicks! kicks! kicks! Tongue jutting out here and there, beaming with joy…yet today we talked with Dr. Stearns about her future. It seems there are no clinical trials open to her (because she is less than a year old and even then— PNET tumors, which hers is classified as, are pretty resistant to treatment). The only real medical option is radiation; but again, her age poses huge risks.

    They will discuss the option of radiation at the tumor board on Thursday, and if the radiologist here at Rainbow is not willing to attempt it, Dr. Stearns believes we could get a second opinion at another hospital.

    However, he did present the option of hospice. He said we could switch our focus to simply enjoying the time we have left. He estimated that if we do nothing, she has four to six months to live. He explained the hospice process (which we could do at home) and told us that children with brain tumors typically "do well until they don't." He said they usually have only mild symptoms until suddenly the tumor becomes too large. Then there is a rapid decline. How I'm writing this, I have not a clue—I believe I've cried all my tears out for the day. My head aches from crying, my heart throbs with pain. That this is my life is unbelievable to me.

And yet I hope in my Father—He will heal her unless there is some greater good that could come no other way. He knows my pain—after all, He had to watch His only Son suffer brutally and die without raising His almighty hand to stop it in order to bring about great good for us. It was this very act that has removed the sting of death for us. No matter what, I will never lose Colette. It would merely be a separation for a time…then sweet, everlasting eternity. Oh, praise God for this!

July 11, 2018, Wednesday

Last evening we were able to bring Colette home from the hospital. Every corner of my home now breaks my heart for it reminds me of old dreams—dreams that have been forsaken for nightmares. I feel like Lucy on the island where dreams come true—not day-dreams but the most horrific nightmares [reference to Chronicles of Narnia's *Voyage of the Dawn Treader*]. *And yet there comes that soft voice of Aslan saying "Courage, dear heart." It comes when I get a kiss from TJ, Tim holds my hand, I feel Colette's soft cheek against mine, or I'm out in nature. God has not, nor will He leave me here.*

Today we set off to enjoy the sun by hiking at the Rocky River Metroparks. It was a perfect sun-filled morning. It is a gift I will choose to cherish.

God, help me.

July 12, 2018, Thursday

If it weren't for the sovereignty of God, I could not bear this. Today the tumor board will meet to discuss Colette. We will hear their thoughts tomorrow at the outpatient clinic. What peace there is in knowing that my good, wise Father—Who is orchestrating all this—was in that meeting "turning hearts whatever way He wishes" [referring to Prov. 21:1].

Meanwhile, we continue to soak in the beauty of these days. Colette could not be more loved or more happy. Just a whimper brings us all rushing to her aid—including TJ who always brings back her smiles with his sweet reassurances, "It's okay—we will take care of you!" he tells her. And we will!

After this, I will read my Bible and pray—seeking my Father's comfort for the night. A night that would be unendurable without Him.

July 13, 2018, Friday

Today we got the plan from Dr. Stearns—I was bursting with anticipation when we arrived at the clinic. So much so that when Dr. Hackney [another wonderful oncologist that had cared for Colette during her months as an inpatient] *came by just to peek at Colette in the waiting room, I peppered her with questions about where she sends patients, how to find clinical trials, etc. She seemed surprised by my questions and inquired why I was asking—apparently, she was at the tumor board meeting herself and, much to my relief, told me that the discussion concerning Colette made no mention of hospice, referrals or trial treatments. She told me that hospice is always an option and a discussion with families merely because it is always an option; and should a family feel that it is right for them, it is offered. Oh, I can't imagine! How far from done we are. I feel like J.P. Jones, "We have not yet begun to fight!"*

Dr. Stearns then came and presented the new plan which includes six weeks of daily proton radiation[18] to the tumor bed. They will have to determine whether the radiation can be done under sedation or if general anesthesia will be needed. Colette will have to remain motionless during radiation and, up to this point, she has not been able to undergo sedation safely. If they can't sedate her, they will have to use general anesthesia. Daily general anesthesia would be difficult but not impossible. Our hope is that sedation will work now that she is older and not as fragile as she was during previous attempts.

Dr. Stearns will order a repeat MRI of the brain in the next week or so to see if the tumor has increased in size. If the tumor has grown large enough for Dr. Tomei [the neurosurgeon] *to operate, she will then attempt to remove the tumor before the radiation begins.*

---

[18] Proton radiation is a relatively new cancer treatment; it is superior to other forms of radiation in that it has greater controllability, meaning that the radiation can be targeted to highly specific areas of the body while leaving healthy surrounding tissue free from harmful radiation. This type of radiation is ideal for young children because the risk of radiating healthy tissue in a growing child is much greater than in adults, especially in the brain. At the time, Rainbow was the first hospital in Ohio to offer this type of treatment. The department was built around the time Colette was born. One more evidence of God's sovereign goodness.

Meanwhile, samples of Colette's tumor will be further tested to see if there are any mutations that could be targeted by specific chemo drugs. If so, more chemotherapy may follow the radiation.

All of this, and my hope remains in God alone. If He wants her to live, nothing can kill her; and if He does not, nothing will save her. How I pray her life would bring Him more glory than her death would.

Oh, God Who can do all things—will You please orchestrate events so that it is her <u>healing</u> that turns eyes to You and glorifies Your name!

July 14, 2018, Saturday

There is really nothing about today that I wish to record. It felt like a monster of rage boiled up within me and ruined the day. "The wise woman builds her house, but the foolish pulls it down with her hands." [Prov. 14:1]. I was a fool today.

Tomorrow, I will begin picking up the pieces.

July 15, 2018, Sunday

Colette is eleven months old today—Oh, what a darling! Last year at this time, I was as impatient as can be to meet her! What a year she has had—what a sweet, strong darling!

She has finished her antibiotics so I am no longer required to be a ninja PICC line accessor (the skills required to set up and remove IV antibiotics during naps and through the night are really quite noteworthy!)

I have decided to have Colette's birthday party this Saturday…major planning to be done!

July 16, 2018, Monday

We have decided to do all we can together with Colette in the next couple of weeks for who knows what lies ahead for us. So to escape the muggy heat today we set sail for the Cleveland Children's Museum!

It is an old Victorian mansion that has been renovated into the best child's play land ever. The basement contains a giant play world with tunnels to climb through, building materials for forts, play food and kitchen nooks! TJ just took off—the building areas seemed to be his favorite. He loved to set up the orange construction cones and wear a real "worker man's" safety vest. Another room was filled with the most incredible water works—pipes, faucets and everything needed to make an ingeniously contained mess. TJ thoroughly enjoyed himself.

Where was Colette you might ask? Just kicking and twirling her little feet enjoying all the action from the safety of her stroller or in my arms. She got to enjoy some mirrors which always make her smile. It was a fun day together.

Tomorrow we plan to go to the Bedford Metroparks.
PS: Have I mentioned that Colette has begun saying "Mama"? How much more does she want me to fall in love with her?

July 18, 2018, Wednesday
Today was the day that Colette was supposed to have her routine MRI—how good God was to let it be done so much earlier! Instead of just being told such horrific news, we have been given a two week advantage. Tim and I are going to meet the radiologist today to discuss treatment plans.

Yesterday, however, was a beautiful day. We went to the Bedford Metroparks to explore—and such discoveries we made!

We found a glorious field of yellow wild flowers filled with birds and butterflies who were delighting in the warm day. We also discovered a river lined with tiny shells that TJ enjoyed hunting down and collecting.

During the little's nap, Tim met with the headmaster of his school in order to resign until November. The demands of daily radiation treatments along with the uncertainty of time we have remaining with Colette has led us to the decision that Tim should no longer split his time between work and home. We now have one focus—our sweet little girl, made more precious by the threat of being taken.

Later
Everyone is all snug in their beds…I wanted to write before slipping into mine as well. As I mentioned earlier, Tim and I took Colette to meet with Dr. Stearns and Dr. Mansur (the radiologist) today.

126

Dr. Stearns said Colette was doing very well and had her PICC line removed. He scheduled her surgery to place her mediport[19] next Wednesday and ordered her brain MRI for Thursday.

We met with Dr. Mansur, the radiologist, next. He seems an extremely kind and gentle doctor. He broke down the risks of radiation for us in the following way:

1. Immediate side effects—skin irritation, fatigue and hair loss in the area receiving radiation (a small portion of which will be permanent)
2. Intermediate side effects—hearing loss, learning/cognitive difficulties as she grows and the risk of a necrotic stroke (which would appear symptomatically or through an MRI several months following treatment)
3. Late side effects—an increased risk for any type of cancer in the radiated area. This risk begins at the ten-year post radiation mark and increases every year with a lifetime risk of 5-10%.

As I listened, the words to the song "In His Keeping" which I read earlier in the day came to mind. There is no chance in the life of a Christian. All things that come into our lives are specially ordered by our good, wise Father. If these risks do actualize, they happen not because of cruel chance but because of a decision made by a loving Father Who will "work all things for good" [Rom. 8:28].

"Whether waking, whether sleeping—
[She] is in His care."[20]

July 22, 2018, Sunday
What a gift yesterday was! After getting the littles up and ready for the day, I left them in Tim's expert care while I set off to join Kayla at Lyssa's house for the convening of Colette's Rainbow Party set-up committee! Everyone went to work to make the party as sweet and memorable as possible. There were rainbow decorations everywhere, and the food was just as colorful! The cake was beyond anything that could be imagined having been donated by a fabulous baker [Three Girls Cupcakes Shoppe] who had heard Colette's story.

---

[19] The mediport would be Colette's new central line. It would be inserted beneath the skin of her chest and would be accessed as needed for blood draws and IV fluid administration.
[20] *"In His Keeping" by Lelia N. Morris*

When the house was bursting with color, we adorned ourselves likewise! Everyone sported bold colors creating a rainbow among ourselves. The entire family along with friends from Rainbow and from church came to celebrate Colette's day.

Colette herself arrived looking beyond adorable in her rainbow tutu (that thankfully made it through the party without a poo-poo). She was carried around and adored by all.

It was a day of thanksgiving for me to God. I think back to the day she was born. I will never forget my first day with Colette, when I fell in love with her. She was, and will ever be, my "good and perfect gift." She has changed my life for the better and has drawn me closer to the Lord more than any other person on earth.

Thank you, Father, for such a gift!

July 25, 2018, Wednesday

Praise God, today went perfectly—the mediport is placed, and Colette is doing well. Tim and I got up and ready at 5:30 AM as quietly as possible, but TJ with his bat-like hearing was soon up and crying at 5:50 AM. When I went to get him, he informed me that "I cryin'" (which is his favorite line at the moment) and that "sun is up." I got him cleaned up and snuggled on the couch, to await the advent of Oma who arrived just after 6:00.

I then had the cruel job of waking Colette, who was sleeping like an angel with her hands wrapped around her head and her little bottom up in the air. In a matter of minutes, a smile appeared on her sleepy little face, and the three of us left.

We got through the PACU routine and left her in the arms of a familiar anesthesiologist. Colette, as usual, did not cry! She has NEVER cried when they have taken her back…God must always equip her with peace and courage. Oh, to be like her!

Tim and I went outside where we separated so he could get some breakfast for us, and I could discover the beauty of Wade Pond on an early summer morning. For the record, it was everything peaceful and wonderful.

We then had breakfast together and slowly made our way back to the hospital. Before long, Colette was out of surgery and doing well. The mediport is on her left side three inches or so below her underarm.

We took her home where she spent most of the rest of the day sleeping (as did TJ who was thoroughly exhausted by his morning with Oma!). They are both in bed now. Tomorrow is the MRI. What will God do? I am still praying that the tumor will be miraculously gone.

July 26, 2018, Thursday

God has decided not to remove her tumor. How much good must be in store that He would refuse such an opportunity to glorify His name? I must believe this—I must believe that God heard my prayers but out of His wisdom and goodness, has allowed, not only the tumor to remain, but to grow significantly larger. For it has grown so large that now surgery is required.

Stepping back though, we had a good morning. TJ went to Grampy and Grammy's around 11 o'clock, then Tim and I took Colette to the sedation unit. She was able to be sedated without any complications (which is an answer to prayer because now Colette will be able to receive her radiation under sedation rather than under general anesthesia) and taken for the MRI.

When we got the call that she was on her way back to the sedation unit, we were by Wade Pond. We rushed back and arrived just as they entered the unit. Dr. Stearns was in the room waiting for us. He did not wait long to tell us that the tumor had grown substantially (from the size of a grain of rice to the size of a grape). Dr. Tomei was on her way to talk with us. Surgery was already scheduled for Tuesday, July 31st (nine months to the day from her first surgery).

Dr. Stearns told us that the surgery will be helpful because it will remove all visible tumor which will increase the effectiveness of radiation. So it isn't necessarily bad news, just sad news, especially because I so badly wanted God to do a miracle. I wanted to see with my own eyes a supernatural-no-other-explanation miracle. But I must believe that God has a better plan. There is a tiny, tiny poisonous thought in me that whispers "What if you're wrong? What if there is no God, and you are just making this all up. There is no miracle because there is no God…"—that thought will be crushed. I will have faith for I <u>know</u> there is a God. The supernatural-no-other-explanation miracle that I see now is the peace He has given me in the midst of this nightmare.

July 27, 2018, Friday

Another sweet day with our little family. What else can I do but savor these days— each snuggle, each look, each smile. For the first time in my life, I have no plans. I have no desire to foretell my future. I have only today; and I have only to trust my sovereign, good Father. I am limp in His hands.

Kayla came over this morning and joined us for a day at the zoo. What I didn't realize was that Kevin, Lyssa and their children were there as well! What a surprise! We joined them, and TJ and Miller had a merry time while Colette was reintroduced to the incredible wild animals.

Tomorrow we will celebrate Colette's birthday with the Piazza family—roll out the rainbows part two! During nap time I began the process of making Colette's six-layered rainbow birthday cake! A layer for every color in the rainbow…tomorrow it will be frosted and sprinkled!

July 29, 2018, Sunday

Yesterday was another beautiful day with Colette. The cake came together splendidly, and although the birthday girl refused to have any part of it, her guests did it justice. The house was full of people that love her, and there is nothing more special than that!

Today Tim and TJ went to church while Colette and I stayed home. I had a wonderful time with my heavenly Father while Colette was taking her nap. How badly I wanted some time with Him before the surgery on Tuesday.

Oh, how wonderful God is—how good He is! How I love to be His child. There is so much peace in trusting His sovereignty, goodness, and wisdom.

Later during TJ's nap, Colette and I took a walk, enjoying the breezy day, then followed it up with some time in the swing (which always makes her smile!). Before returning to the house, we "toured the gardens" which, though tiny, are still full of exciting discoveries. She is now down for her second nap…

July 30, 2018, Monday

My mind circles around, going from fear of tomorrow to faith in God's sovereignty, wisdom and goodness. Back and forth it goes. Put off fear; put on trust. "What time I am afraid, I will trust in Thee" [Psalm 56:3].

Regardless of the turmoil in my mind, the morning was filled with special moments. We spent our time together at the Rocky River Metroparks, which was lovely as usual.

During TJ's nap, Noopur, a resident doctor from Rainbow who has become a friend, came to spend time with Colette and I. Afterwards, Pastor and Beth [his wife] came to pray.

There I go again! The minute I stop writing the battle starts up again. "What time I am afraid, I will trust in Thee"! Whatever happens tomorrow is a cup prepared for me by my Father—Who controls all things, knows all things and loves me more than anyone on earth. Why should I fear bringing the cup to my lips?

July 31, 2018, Tuesday

Colette is back in surgery now. Oh, the peace of knowing that the events of the day have been carefully and lovingly dictated by my Father—there is no chance involved!

Colette woke up jabbering away at 2:30 this morning. I snuck in on all fours to turn off her feeds at 3:00 AM hoping that if she didn't see me she would go back to sleep. My little Colette had no such plans. I got her at 3:45, and she was up for good! Tim and I enjoyed some sweet laughs and snuggles with her, and I got her dressed for the day. We had a big egg and toast breakfast then left the house around 5:15 AM when my parents arrived to watch TJ.

It was so hard leaving our home. My heart ached with the unspeakable fear—the "what if." But I can't even write it. If it happens, there will be grace. God will be by my side, comforting me and strengthening me. The problem with my imagination is that there is no filter of God's grace on it—the events are not properly shaded with God's comfort intertwined. I look ahead and see only the possible sorrow and pain. I cannot see the supernatural peace and love that God has promised to surround me with should the "what if" happen. God does not give us grace before we need it. We must simply trust that if our moment of need arrives, His grace will be there and all will be well.

Pastor Pete came to pray with us before they took Colette back, and Allison stopped by to see her as well (after working her night shift in the NICU). Lastly, Dr. Tomei came to reiterate the plan for surgery; by 7:30 AM, Colette was taken to the OR. We all wait. And pray.

Later [6:00 PM]

Colette is back with us—still intubated and on a ventilator, but she is back! Per Dr. Tomei, she did "swimmingly!" She said she was easily able to distinguish the tumor which made the removal easier. She also told us that Colette barely even bled and required no blood transfusions! The post-surgery MRI showed no tumor remaining and no evidence of a stroke (which had been a surgical risk).

My favorite statement by Dr. Tomei, however, was: "Now that it is out, she'll have radiation, and she should be good." Of course, she doesn't know the future, but aren't those words so sweet? I will savor them for days.

They will take the breathing tube out shortly.

August 1, 2018, Wednesday

Colette did very well through the night. She is a little more swollen around the incision site, but it otherwise looks good. She will most likely be moved to the oncology floor today! Honestly, her biggest issue right now is itchiness from the Dilaudid she is getting for pain.

August 2, 2018, Thursday

Colette did so well last night! We got moved to Mac 6 around 10:00 PM, and she was soon settled and asleep with only one rough patch from pain. She seems much more comfortable today. Tim took over around noon while I took TJ home and spent the rest of the day with him. Dr. Tomei is talking about discharge tomorrow!

August 3, 2018, Friday

Ready to hear something incredible—my entire family is home! Both my babies are napping in their own cribs! Praise God for His amazing kindness to us! Colette continued to do well all day yesterday, and today she was switched to pain medications that could be taken through the G-tube which meant we could go home. The neurosurgery team had already given us their blessing, so we had Colette packed and out of there by 12:30 PM! What a happy moment to bring her through our doors again, to see her sitting in the living room surrounded by a mountain of pillows to soften any tip overs.

God has certainly turned our mourning into joy this week! [Ps. 30:11]

August 4, 2018, Saturday

Although everyone fell asleep in their beds last night, not all of us remained in them! Colette had a difficult night, waking every hour to two hours; then this morning, she vomited twice and had two episodes of blood in her diaper (similar to what she had in the past)!? Also, her swelling at the incision site has not reduced in size…Colette! So many mysteries surround that girl.

She's doing lots of make-up sleeping today.

August 5, 2018, Sunday

   Colette ended up having a third diaper with blood in it which the on-call oncologist wanted to have examined, so into the ER we went for Colette to have her labs checked. All her blood work came back normal, and we were able to return home after about two hours. The ER doctor thought that the vomiting and blood in her diapers could be from a stomach virus. She's been started on medicine for nausea and has been switched to Pedialyte rather than formula. We will see if this helps.

August 7, 2018, Tuesday

   Back at Rainbow. Poor Colette's vomiting has increased, and she has also been more irritable. On top of that, the incision site has gotten increasingly swollen. She has been admitted to the oncology floor and will get a T2 Turbo MRI to quickly check the amount of fluid buildup around the incision site. After determining this, they must figure out what to do with the fluid. Should they simply drain it and wait to see if it returns, or will they need to put in a permanent shunt to drain the fluid from her brain to her stomach?

August 9, 2018, Thursday

   What a busy couple of days! The MRI revealed that there was indeed fluid accumulating in the incision area. Dr. Tomei decided to drain the fluid with a needle in the sedation unit only to have the fluid re-accumulate in about fifteen minutes. She then determined that it was a pseudo-meningocele, which is simply a pocket of cerebrospinal fluid that is not harmful, especially where it is located on Colette. It should not pose a risk during radiation. After that was decided, and after Colette proved that she could tolerate some feeds through her G-tube, she was able to come home last night!

   We returned to Rainbow again this afternoon for Colette's brain and spine MRI...ALL CLEAR! Praise God!

   Oh, thank You God for the gift of more time with Colette!

August 12, 2018, Sunday

   How lovely to think back a year ago...how excited I was. Days away from meeting my Colette. I will always cherish those memories. It was my last bit of perfection—the last time I felt pure joy without any fear or sorrow mingled in. It was beautiful.

These evenings remind me of those nights a year ago—TJ down, Tim asleep…me listening to the glorious August crickets chirping away as I read page after page of whatever enticing book it was at the time.

Colette has transformed one of my least favorite months into one of my favorites. She has sanctified it. What a gift she has to transform everyone and everything she comes in contact with!

Thank you, God, for what we have been given. Thank you for the sweetness of those days.

Thank you for Colette! Thank you that regardless of the future, You will be a fixed presence. You will beautify and sanctify every day, every moment. Thank you God for the wonder of Your immutability in this ever-changing world.

August 13, 2018, Monday

Colette did splendidly on her first day of radiation! We followed all the NPO orders to a "T": stopped Elecare at 6 AM, stopped breast milk at 8 AM, stopped Pedialyte at 10 AM and put the lidocaine cream on Colette to numb the area of her mediport just before she left with Tim.

Tim said she was as good as gold. She didn't cry once, not even during her mediport access! She woke from her sedation giddy, sweet and chatty. They were home by 2:00 in the afternoon.

As for TJ and I, we played outside then ran to Target where we gathered all the necessary equipment for the coming storm…potty training!

We came back with Pull-Ups, undies, and a fascinating little potty that makes a fun siren sound every time you "flush" it! TJ is more than excited to begin this mysterious adventure. We then read books, worked on recognizing numbers, sang the ABCs times a billion and talked about how God created everything (although he kept insisting that "Otto" from the John Deere videos did…his theology is a bit shaky). I made chocolate chip cookies, Cheerio bars, did three loads of laundry and cleaned the bathroom. All in all…a lovely day!

August 14, 2018, Tuesday

 A year ago, I was in the throes of the most agonizing pain…working hard to bring my most precious girl into the world! How thankful I am to have been given an entire year of her! She has now put her tiny fingerprint on every day of the calendar, and I will always have the little smudges she's made to cherish and remember!

 Thank you, God!

August 15, 2018, Wednesday

 Happy Birthday Darling Girl! What a wonderful day we have had. Tim and I took Colette to her outpatient clinic visit with Dr. Stearns while TJ spent the morning with Grammy and Grampy. The wonderful staff at the outpatient clinic had her room completely decorated—and that was only the beginning!

 Her room at radiation was also bedazzled, complete with balloons and presents! An entire group of nurses came on their lunch break to sing her "Happy Birthday"! She was smothered in love.

 Thank you, God, for all this love!

 Back at home, TJ and Colette decided that there was too much to celebrate to waste time napping; therefore, only an hour nap for Colette and a half hour nap for TJ!

 We played and snuggled, and after dinner came the full-out party. TJ "helped" Colette open her gifts (which included hair bows that I can actually get to stay in her tiny bits of hair now!) She loved the pink bear that TJ bought for her…she held each treasure one by one.

 Thank You, God, once more for such an amazing gift…only You could create something so beautiful.

Picture: Happy First Birthday, Colette! For the record, the cake was smeared not eaten…

CHAPTER 13

New Mountains to Climb

The remaining days of August were spent in acclimating to new routines and new ways of life. Tim continued his leave of absence from work and undertook the responsibility of taking Colette to and from her radiation treatments every day. These days started early and stealthily as I would wake every morning at six to tiptoe cat-like into Colette's nursery to shut off her over-night feed and begin her breast milk feed. The adrenaline rush one benefits from when tasked with silently creeping on a baby's creaking hardwood floor every morning really sets one up for the rest of the day! If I made it through my ritual without prematurely waking Colette, the house would remain silent until she and TJ would wake around 7:30-8:00 when I would then shut off her breast milk feed and start giving her Pedialyte.

This entire process was a balancing act between giving her enough fluids and calories to maintain hydration and adequate nutrition while avoiding over-taxing Colette's stomach and causing her to vomit (and lose all the hydration/nutrition we had worked so hard to get in her!). This balance, which had always been difficult for Colette, was now doubly so as sedation/radiation had reduced the amount of time that we could spread out her eating/drinking. Her stomach had to be completely empty before she could be sedated (in order to avoid negative side effects). This was the reason for the very specific feed regime. Certain things could be given up to specific times. We followed it all with military-style promptness. By nine in the morning, Tim and Colette set off for Rainbow.

Their days together at radiation became a garden of memories for Tim to cherish. Every day was the same—same toys, same care teams at sedation/radiation, and the same joy of togetherness. Colette sailed through these early days of radiation. The procedure itself lasted only a couple of minutes. The majority of the time was spent in preparation.

Every Monday she would have her mediport accessed (a needle and tubing inserted; it would remain this way until taken out on Friday). The sedation team would then attach her monitors and prepare for her sedation. Once the team was ready, she was sedated while in Tim's arms then gently placed on the bed. The team would then take her to Proton Therapy where she would be flipped onto her belly, face perfectly aligned by a premade mask that held her in the position needed for treatment. Once she was settled, the proton radiation would begin.

After only a couple of minutes, the radiation team would give the "all clear," and she would be taken to a recovery room where she would wake up—giggling and jabbering in her dazed state. She and Tim would then attend any other scheduled appointments for the day before heading back home. The routine may sound grim for a child, but what I did not record was the kisses, the toys and the kindness that every member of the team showered on our girl every day. Though the procedure was scientific, the method was filled with tender love.

As for TJ and I, we were settling into a new routine ourselves! Our home was returning to familiar form after months of neglect. Familiar smells filled the kitchen, and familiar books were pulled out and read. I delighted in the beauty of being home. It was during these weeks that TJ and I embarked on one of the greatest adventures a three-year-old can have: potty training. With the help of Skittles, fancy underpants and an incredible new potty, we kissed diapers farewell and entered the big-boy world of underwear.

Towards the end of August, we hosted a blood drive with the help of our church through the American Red Cross in honor of Colette's birthday. Countless times had I watched bags of blood products flow into our little girl, each unit of blood linked with a selfless donor. I could not forget what strangers had done to help my daughter survive her first year of life. Hosting a blood drive seemed to be the perfect way to give back. With the help of Colette's army of supporters, we were able to collect 150 units of blood that day.

Through it all, our home was a happy one, and these summer days were being savored.

On August 28, 2018, I wrote:

What blissful summer days we have had! Grammy and Grampy have opened their new pool! Between them and Kevin and Lyssa, we have become quite the aquatic creatures! This is especially true as the weather has been quite toasty—90s the past two days!

Colette's treatments are going well; we've just now begun noticing some minor hair loss and redness in the treatment area (we are 11 out of 30 treatments in). She is thriving though. She has mastered sitting and rolling...now working on transitioning from sitting to lying. She is ever so vocal, babbling most of the day! As for eating, the past three days have been her best yet. I have been putting food on my finger or on toothettes [little foam swabs that became our friends during our days at Rainbow], *and she has done really well. I have even gotten small pieces of yogurt melts and puffs in her mouth!*

The following day I record the update we were given at Colette's weekly outpatient clinic appointment:

Colette got a very good report from Dr. Gold, her neurologist. She said, "It is nothing short of amazing how well she is doing!" She is so pleased that Colette's made so much progress so quickly. She said Colette has hypotonia [weakened muscle tone] *which she will most likely have all her life, but through strengthening her core muscles, it will not hinder her in any way. She said she believes Colette will be up on all fours in the next two months and walking by the time she is two. The thought of Colette being two made me cry...could it be? I will leave it to the One Who "does all things well" [Mark 7:37]. She also said she will try to take Colette off Keppra* [her seizure medication] *after her MRI scan in October.*

Through all the joy, there remained that dark day in the future: the day of the MRI scan which hovered in late October. We had no definite date yet, but we knew it was out there, the window through which we would gaze into our future...one of sorrow or one of extended hope.

Still, that day was far off, and what we had learned through our journey with Colette was to avoid the temptation to allow potential sadness to

139

rob present joy. Thus, on a wave of optimism, we entered into September. A month that would bring new change but of a pleasantly different variety.

We had lived in our home in Cleveland for six years and had every intention of remaining there for the near future. The uncertainties surrounding Colette caused every rational fiber in our bodies to resist any thought of moving. And yet, in September the thought "It is time to move" not only entered our heads, but grew feet and arms and legs and turned our world upside down. No doubt to our nearest and dearest, our actions that month were as frightening as they were astonishing, but our actions have since proved to be one of God's greatest blessings to us. In any case, on September 1st we had no thought of moving; on September 15th, we had a "For Sale" (by owner, if you do not already think we were mad enough) sign perched in our front yard. In the interim we had found ourselves a realtor and were earnestly searching for a home further from the city, nearer our parents and closer to our church.

September 13, 2018, Thursday, records a hint of the upheaval that entered our home during this month along with the reassurance that even in the midst of chaos we had not lost sight of our most precious gift.

The saga continues…Yesterday was an exhausting day. Tim took both littles to Rainbow for Colette's appointment while my mom and I painted the bathroom, entrance way and dining room—what a transformation! Today, we plan to list the house! Dear, sweet Meadowbrook!

Meanwhile…Colette.

Is she an angel? She is without a doubt the most prim, lady-like one year old I have ever met. She has this sweet little lips-closed smile that is so coy it is maddening! I can see her doing it now in my mind! Oh, it makes me cry—how dear she is. She could not be more lovable nor more loved. I sing her an old Patch the Pirate song before bed each night. I've modified it a bit, but it is perfect:

"*You're special to Jesus,*
There's no one else like you,
I wouldn't trade you for anyone else—
You're special, you see,

140

God has prepared a plan,
He wants You to do.
You're special,
You're special to the Lord."

After our home was listed, our days returned to a more manageable flow of Tim and Colette going to radiation, and TJ and I lost in the tiny, quiet world of home. The only addition was daily online home searches and occasional viewings of the houses that particularly piqued our interest.

September 19, 2018, Wednesday

Colette is down to four more radiation treatments. Dr. Mansur saw her today and said she is doing "remarkable"—no skin break down, no weight loss and she's even making steps in development! He also said (though we know he is merely human and has no ability to foretell the future) that "this should do the trick." This brought me to tears. He has no idea what a treasure his words are. They are oxygen to hope that has been dying for the want of air.

Dr. Stearns said she is doing fabulous from his perspective. Following her last treatment on Tuesday, he will see her, then give us a month off! No visits, no therapies, just time home until her MRI. That being the case, we booked a vacation to Colonial Williamsburg for October 11-17th! I bought "fall bounce" tickets which give us access to both Colonial Williamsburg and Busch Gardens amusement park! Basically…it will be a glorious time—one final celebration before lifting the veil to view our future at the MRI.

On September 21st, just a week after listing our home, we received and accepted our first offer. The first piece of the puzzle had fallen into place. Four days later, we celebrated another glorious event:

September 25, 2018, Tuesday

Colette has finished radiation! Praise God He has borne her through—once again He has made her a "wonder unto many" [Ps. 71:7]. She had no major complications, and she is thriving! She "has a rhythm inside her," as Dr. Stearns says. She just moves, moves, moves. Every day she is gaining ground, and how we thank and praise our God.

She finished treatments around noon with all her wonderful nurses and doctors present who have been with her every step of the way. There was so much love in the room. Colette is perhaps "unfortunate" when compared with other children her age when it comes to her diagnosis and prognosis. But in one area she is more fortunate than almost anyone on earth, she is rich in love. I know of no one more loved, more prayed for than her. What a sweet, incredible little girl. What a mighty, good God! If there is a God to be trusted, it is Him— if there is a God to be worshiped, it is Him. If there is peace to be had, it is through Him. Thank you God for the past three months…what a gift!

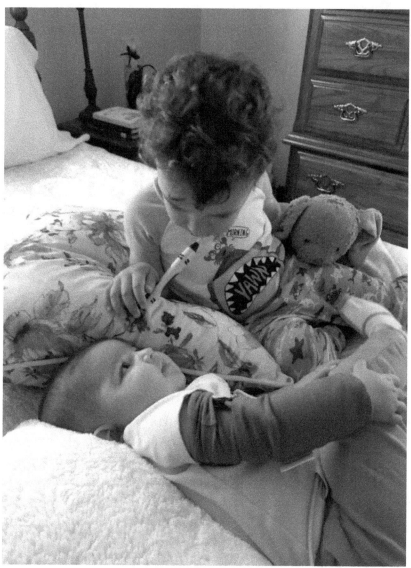

Picture: TJ and Colette…the sweetest of friends

The next day, I began a new journal with the following words:

September 26, 2018, Wednesday

I used to be a girl who planned—who dreamed with a checklist in my hands. I had a plan for the month—a goal for the year and stepping stones for the years to come. I am no longer that girl. When I gaze ahead—even one day from now—everything is misty. I have come to a time in my life where I am truly learning what it means to "walk by faith, not by sight" [2 Cor. 5:7]. I am learning to have peace not because I "know" and can "control" the future but because I trust the goodness of the One Who truly knows and controls the future.

I have no idea what these pages will hold—pain or joy; yet every time I take up my pen to record, peace will be available to me because it is my good, loving, wise Father that dictates the events of the day. When I remember this—I can, no matter how painful the circumstances—have peace.

October was a "honeymoon" month for us. Colette's radiation treatments were complete, and she had no scheduled therapies or appointments. The month was dedicated strictly to being together—to lapping up every sweet moment before the upcoming MRI scan. Tim was to return to work after our vacation in the middle of October, and the days leading up to this vacation were filled with family moments. Simple things such as taking both of the children grocery shopping with me became grand milestones that would fill my eyes with tears. We spent as much of our time outdoors as possible relishing the beauty of fall.

The hunt for a home continued, but soon reached a happy ending. On October 6th we spotted a house online that looked idealistic. That evening we stashed the littles in the car and set off to view the house that would become our beloved home. We made an offer that evening which was accepted within a couple of days. The family that we bought the home from was moving ten doors down, *that* family was moving across the street and THAT family was having a home built that would not be ready until mid December. We would not be able to take possession of the home until the beginning of January. Even in this, God poured out His blessing. The lady buying our home agreed to wait until January to move into our house, thus allowing us to spend one final Christmas at our dear little house on Meadowbrook.

Having this settled, we were able to make our way down to Williamsburg, Virginia with hearts fully focused on only one thing—each other!

Our trip truly was one of the greatest weeks we spent together as a family. Colonial Williamsburg had always been a favorite spot for Tim and I; it became even more so as we shared it with our children. We toured the beautiful Revolutionary City, Colette on my hip and TJ tumbling through every garden and shop with a vivid curiosity. We also spent a couple of days at Busch Gardens learning TJ's fearless nature when it came to rides and roller coasters and allowing Colette to watch the buzzing flow of colors and people. At Jamestown, TJ explored like a renegade sailor on the ships. What his mind did not grasp of this historic trip, his hands certainly did. He made himself at home in the "wigglewams" of the Indian village and was fascinated by the armor and guns of the soldiers.

While on this trip I wrote:

October 15, 2018, Monday

Colette is fourteen months today! What a gloriously sweet fourteen-month-old she is—thank you Father for letting us have her for fourteen months! Thank you for the golden memories I can always cherish…many of which are being collected this week.

We went to Williamsburg this morning—it was a hot one! It was in the 80s today and certainly felt like a summer day. We toured the Governor's Palace, and TJ was thrilled with the gardens. We made several other stops including one at the market place where TJ finally got his tricorn hat and Colette her little bonnet! By noon the littles were done, and we took them to the condo for nap time. I feel like my soul is dancing here—I find it hard to believe I'm not flying. And the sweetest thought is—that Heaven must be better! I am not sure what Heaven is like, but it has to be better. And if this is true…ahhh! What bliss that I will one day live there!

When the littles wake we will take them swimming, then baths and bed…tomorrow we will take a jaunt into the 1600s—Jamestown!

It was on this vacation that Colette began to crawl. We had the unmistakable pleasure of catching her distances from the spot we placed her. By the end of the week the blankets we lined the condo floor with to allow her to play were useless—our girl was on the move! It was one final, lasting memento of our trip!

However, one voicemail message received while on our trip gave us a concrete date to dread; Dr. Stearns's medical assistant called telling us that Colette's MRI was scheduled for October 26th. With this dark cloud perched before us, we returned from our vacation and picked up our lives at home. Tim returned to work, and I savored the chance of having both littles to myself. Although all felt so normal and all looked so well, a postscript on my October 21st entry gives a peek into the undertow of fear that was ever present.

PS: For the record, Friday is looming dark and terrible in the background of every thought.

We celebrated TJ's birthday early, determined to give him his special day before any threatening storm could break to rob him of his birthday just as it had done the previous year with Colette's initial diagnosis.

On October 23, 2018, Tuesday, I wrote:

It seems so strangely like a replay of last year. The scan is coming Friday, and today we went to my mom's for the day just like we did a year ago. Colette was even sleeping when we arrived, just as she was last year. Mom and I played with TJ outside while peeking in on Colette as she slept, again, just like last year. The battle of fear versus trust grows more intense, but I must remind myself that there is something else that is the same as last year: my God, the author of the future. Oh, Katie what do you have to fear?

He has promised only to allow good into your life. He has promised it would never be "too much." He has promised never to leave you for a moment. Is it death you so desperately cower from—it has been defeated. The sting is now gone. Death is no longer an exit but an entranceway to something far sweeter, far more beautiful than you could ever imagine. It does not bring with it separation and hopelessness, but eternal, secure togetherness. No longer fear, Katie. Have faith. This is true. These days, these moments are temporary. What will it matter one hundred million years from now if I was made, for the sake of God's glory and the good of the kingdom, to be separated from her for sixty years or so? By that time, every loss will be more than restored.

Praise God what a hope! Praise Christ what a gift!

Thank you God for removing that horrible sting. Thank You for the promises whereby I can live without fear.

A couple of days later, on the evening before Colette's MRI I wrote:

Oh, the joy of having such a God. I feel as though everywhere I turn, I hear His voice of comfort. I know He is answering the prayers of His people. Verses and songs are flooding my mind. It is true that peace is always available to the believer. We need only look at our Father, and our souls once quaking with fear grow still. Furthermore, joy is ever an option: "In His presence is fullness of joy" [Psalm 16:11].

I don't know what my next entry will record, but it will be good news. For He has promised He will never withhold good from me, and He will use every detail of my life for His glory and my good.

I feel as though I am intoxicated with the joy of knowing Him and trusting Him. What a gift, what richness to be His beloved child. I can fully rest in His loving disposal of my future.

Blessed be the name of the Lord.

October 26, 2018, Friday
Praise God! No tumor! No tumor! No tumor!

Praise our wonderful Lord! Colette did so well for the procedure. They ended up doing a whole brain and spine MRI plus a lumbar puncture. The scans showed nothing of suspicion! The lumbar puncture results will be available on Monday, but Dr. Stearns believes they will be negative. All I can think is that this means two more months! This means <u>real</u> smiles for Thanksgiving, Christmas and New Years…By God's grace the bittersweet memories of this season last year will be replaced with pure sweet memories.

It was difficult being at Rainbow. Especially before the results. Every corner of that place holds shadows of my former self—weary, fearful, but hopeful Katie. The hallways— which my feet had traveled all hours, all seasons—contained echoes of conversations. I lived there. I watched the seasons pass there; how difficult it was to go back…one year from the time we first came. How painful to be handed an ID pass with my picture emblazoned on the front. The picture that was taken a year ago just moments after being told of "the mass." Seeing the shell-shocked face and those haunted eyes flooded me with memories. A closer look at the picture revealed that not only was I wearing the same look of terror as I was a year ago, I was also wearing the very same shirt!

146

But God has brought us out of that miry pit and has set our feet on the sturdy ground.

Thank you God for this day of miracles!

The surge of emotional relief that followed this news cannot be described. All the tension, all the emotional and spiritual armor that I had been burying myself under could be released; those days were marked by tears running down a smiling face. All is well…all is well…seemed to be the oxygen we breathed.

Still, we had many painful one-year anniversaries to get through—many dates and many triggers that made our souls quake with the agony of their memory. It is strange that even now, fall—the rustling of leaves, the deep, dark blue of the sky, the sight of pumpkins and mums—tosses me back to those early days of Colette's diagnosis. But that fall was not a time to sorrow, for we had HER…and all things were being made new.

October 29, 2018, Monday

We've passed the one year mark. One year ago yesterday it all began. All I can say is thank You God for Your faithfulness, Your grace, and now Your blessing. We have come through the deep waters; and we have arrived at a beautiful place. We have scars. We are no longer the people, the family we were before. But thank you God for the scars, for it was through the scarring that we have been made more like You. We suffered. You suffered. We bear the marks. You bear the marks. Through You, no agony will be wasted.

Today was filled with blessings. We had another morning together—the littles and I. Colette woke up from her afternoon nap prematurely and allowed me to rock her back to sleep in my arms…treasure!

After nap time I took the littles to Kevin and Lyssa's Trick or Treat party with tears of gratitude in my eyes. It was a night filled with sugar, laughter and plenty of fun. Tim surprised the kids by showing up in a giant eagle costume delivering candy!

Oh, my wonderful Father—Thank You!

Thank You for the storm, and thank You now for this. How I love this gift—how good You are to me. Thank You.

On October 31st we remembered the amazing feat that God had brought Colette through a year ago that day—a fourteen-hour brain surgery on her little eleven-week-old body. We praised God again for His loving care and returned to Rainbow PICU, this time voluntarily, bringing candy for the staff. Colette was dressed appropriately as Wonder Woman, for she certainly exemplified Psalm 71:7—a "wonder" unto many.

CHAPTER 14

All Is Calm. All Is Bright

U nder the guidance of Dr. Stearns, we decided to continue Colette's
treatments with a low dose chemotherapy regimen that could be
given through her G-tube while she remained at home. She would
receive this chemotherapy one week out of the month for the next
six months. Dr. Stearns believed that if some small amount of tumor had
survived the surgery and radiation, this chemotherapy could potentially destroy or slow its growth. The risks associated with the drugs were not as great
as the risks of the chemotherapy she had received a year earlier; still she would
remain at risk for infections and would require twice a month visits to the
outpatient clinic where her lab work could be monitored. There was a potential for nausea, vomiting and diarrhea; but the hopes were that these side
effects would be mild enough to manage at home while allowing her to live
as normal of a life as possible. She began this treatment in early November.

November 5, 2018, Monday

*Colette began round one of her new chemo regimen. A home healthcare nurse came
out this morning to make sure I was administering the two drugs correctly, but after today
I will be on my own. It went smoothly. I put TJ up in his crib with toys telling him, "It's
Coco's medicine time. You play until I am done then I will come get you!" He accepted
without a fuss! (I didn't want any mishaps with him around while I mixed and prepared
the chemo!) I then put Colette in her high chair with toys and other distractions. With the*

littles secured, I put on a mask, gown and double gloves. Finally, I set up a station on the countertop where I opened the medicine capsules and released the powder into my prepared apple juice (per instructions…I am not sure what is so magical about apple juice, but I believe it has something to do with the taste for those taking the medicine by mouth. Not going to affect Colette, but I'm not risking anything!) I stirred the mixture then pulled it up in a syringe and gave it to Colette through her G-tube. After it was given, I carefully disposed of all the waste materials.

Finally, TJ and Colette were released from their imposed prisons—all happy and unalarmed. I repeated the procedure an hour later when I had to give the second chemotherapy medication (they are supposed to be given an hour apart.)

So far Colette has had no signs of nausea, vomiting or diarrhea. The only other changes I've had to make is wearing gloves for diaper changes as, apparently, the drug is excreted in the urine. It is incredible to think that such a powerful drug can be given right at home to a fourteen-month-old, and the world goes on without a blink.

As I give it, I just pray for God to bless it. I think of that verse in Psalm 127:1— "Unless the Lord builds the house, they labor in vain who build it. Unless the Lord guards the city, the watchman stays awake in vain."

Unless God blesses this process, it will all be for nothing.

Please, Lord.

Picture: Mommy mixing chemo in the kitchen

It was during this time that Colette was switched from her formula based food to a whole food blend that was recommended by a new dietician. The new blend could go through the pump into her G-tube and had a tremendous impact on her GI problems. We were thrilled to see her vomiting decrease; and whether linked with this change or not, we had the utter joy of watching her barriers to eating start to come down. The one year anniversary of her second brain surgery was marked by the advent of this new wonder.

November 7, 2018, Wednesday

Praise God for the miracle He performed a year ago today during Colette's second craniotomy! Not done working miracles, God did another nearly miraculous thing! Colette took her first bite of food! Willingly! Desirously! She took an animal cracker from Tim then put it in her mouth—for the next hour she sucked on it, gnawed on it, and filled her parents with joy with it! She did it again in the evening, and this morning, she gnawed twice on a graham cracker! It is simply incredible to see her with food in her hands—Thank you God!

It was an autumn marked by the blossoming of Colette. A complete opposite of the year before. I wrote later:

In every way she is thriving. She is learning to crawl on her hands and knees, and if it weren't for our slippery wood floors, I think she would be mastering this skill in a week or two. Meanwhile, she continues her "army crawl" and is the speediest little slug you ever saw! She has also begun pulling herself up to a high kneeling position. She says the word "Coco" which sounds angelic, but the cherry on top is her eating! Today when I took the littles grocery shopping, I handed them both animal crackers, and that darling Colette immediately put hers into her mouth! It makes me cry just thinking about it! Praise God for these amazing breakthroughs!

The week following Colette's first round of new chemotherapy proved to be a difficult one. The diarrhea, that had been mentioned as a possible side effect, began in earnest and left Colette weak and listless. The memories stirred by her limp, exhausted body spending the majority of her day in my arms were painful; but with sleep, snuggles and gentle rehydration, we soon began to "*see our old Colette peeking through her tired eyes.*" We learned through this round and were prepared with counter measures for the subsequent rounds. By Thanksgiving, she had all her lovable "Colettishness" back, and we spent a beautiful time with our families—giving thanks to the God Who had made all our joy possible.

December was a month of preparation. We prepared to move. We prepared for Christmas, and we prepared for the next MRI scan that sat glowering at us on the calendar: January 10th. Still, we did our best to focus on the joy that was right before us. There really is nothing like December in a home filled with children. We delighted in our advent calendar, made sugar cookies and added a ruby red slipper ornament to the tree in honor of Colette's first Christmas at home (it is true, there really is "no place like home"!)

On December 11, 2018, Tuesday I wrote:

I could cry any minute of the day with joy and love and thankfulness for these days I've been given. From the moment TJ and Colette wake, we jump right into our beautiful, sweet routines. We move slowly, make lots of messes and talk A LOT! It is glorious.

During this month, Colette embarked on round two of her chemotherapy which went flawlessly thanks to a new medication that prevented diarrhea. She continued to make small advances with regards to "eating" which really was more sucking on crackers than eating. But seeing Colette with something in her mouth was miracle enough for us! She began pulling herself up to a standing position which meant that it was finally time to lower the mattress in her crib…one more tangible evidence that our girl was blossoming.

Just before Christmas, we bundled up the littles along with a shocking amount of sugary sweets to make a pilgrimage back to Rainbow. We made stops at all of the departments that had played such an enormous role in Colette's life and shared our Christmas joy with our beloved friends and heroes.

December 24, 2018, Monday

It's Christmas Eve! What a beautiful time—such a mixture of joy, anticipation, thankfulness and awe fills me. How beautiful it is to feast on the victories of this past year. Colette is HERE, home, and thriving! That darling girl could not be more beautiful in her appearance or her personality. Her little coos and smiles…she melts me into tears of amazement and love daily.

Today she astounded us all by eating tiny spoonfuls of Oma's fruit salad—one mouthful after another! Then proceeded to gnaw on crackers and puffs. Who is this Wonder Woman?

I see her, and I see the power of my God. Blessed be His name. What a God to entrust one's life to; what a God to serve.

Our Christmas was spent with family and filled with the celebration of the birth of our wonderful Savior. The new year brought us to our final days at Meadowbrook. The last minute packing was accomplished under the indefatigable supervision of Tim who was off work for Christmas break. We moved to our new home on Beech Lane (which I swiftly renamed "Beech Loveliness," finding it much more descriptive of its virtues) on January 3rd. Two days later I wrote:

We are still glorying in the beauty of this home! Tim and I just can't get over how much we love it, and how amazed we are to be living here. The first morning we woke here, TJ asked me if we were going anywhere; when I replied we were not, he answered, "Good, let's stay here a long time." That's just how I feel too.

We had the boxes unpacked and the house in order by the time Tim returned to work. It was not long before we felt very much at home. It was a blessing that we felt so at home in this new house, for once again we were bracing ourselves for what could be a life-altering scan. Through the holidays we could distract ourselves with the bliss that was dancing right before us; by January 9th there was nowhere else to turn. We had to look directly at the thing that terrified us most. It had come. But I had walked along this precipice before, and I knew what to do…or at least Who to turn to.

January 9, 2018, Wednesday

I've come to another night before my world may shatter. I don't know what my next entry will be, but there is peace to be had. When I stop writing I will open the Bible and renew my mind. I will drink the Living Water that will quench my thirst for security and safety. We are perfectly safe in His hands.

It was joy, not sorrow that came the following day…

Praise the Lord—no tumor! Praise God Who hears and answers prayers, Who is merciful and gracious to us! Praise our glorious Father!

Victorious

It all went perfectly. Colette sedated quickly and easily and was back before we knew it—full of chatter and smiles. After about an hour Dr. Stearns came through the door with a thumbs up saying "Scans look good!" Bliss.

Praise God our home is still a house of radiant joy.

CHAPTER 15

A Cup of Joy

n the days that followed that January MRI scan, I enjoyed sipping from the cup of joy my God had handed me. Our home became a "normal" home. I took care of the littles, Tim worked, and we rejoiced in a season of reprieve. I began Colette's third round of chemotherapy which once again went smoothly. Colette continued to make grounds in every area of development. Having moved to a new county, she was enrolled in a new division of Help Me Grow. Colette was assigned both a physical therapist and an occupational therapist that would come to our home weekly to work with her. Colette's former occupational therapist, Mary, who had worked so diligently with Colette during her many months of stubborn stagnation, continued to visit us although on a friendship basis rather than a professional one. Mary remained one of Colette's dearest friends—the one who disguised therapy so well as play that Colette did not realize she should detest it. Colette's new therapists picked up where Mary had left off and built on her budding skills. By the end of the month Colette had begun taking (tiny) drinks out of a sippy cup and could sign the words for "all done" and "more." She was promptly dubbed "Little Miss Unstoppable."

On January 26, 2018, Saturday, I wrote my final entry in yet another journal saying:

When I began this journal, my future lay before me opaque and unsettling. The days have passed—unfolding perfectly according to my Father's will and how glorious they have been! Two miraculously clean scans, a magical trip to Williamsburg, a picture-perfect Christmas, a move to a "more than you could ask or think" (Eph 3:20) home, and the blossoming of Colette. She has begun to crawl, stand and EAT! Every day I have been surrounded by God's faithful love and goodness. Praise God for the beauty of these four months.

Now I look once more ahead—to a future uncertain, yet under the control of the same good Father.

These past couple of days I have felt myself starting to hope again. Tears come to my eyes as I write this because it hurts so badly. It is so terrifying to let the thoughts begin to grow...but what if. What if she lives. Is it wrong for me to fear hoping? Because oh, how I want to shield my heart, to build such a thick fortress around it so that no flood of sorrow can overwhelm it. I shrink from hope, and yet I question is that wrong?

But the answer has come to me, I believe God does not command us to hope in a particular outcome; He commands us to hope in Him. To trust <u>Him</u>. And I do—what time I am afraid, I have learned to trust in Him.

February came, and with it the happy discovery that Colette's hair (though thinning from chemotherapy) was now long enough for tiny pigtails (much to TJ's delight!) We spent most of our days cooped up inside the walls of our Beech Loveliness, and though the days were still and quiet outside, our home was bustling. Colette acquired skills daily with the help of her wonderful therapists and the assistance of her older, active brother (who seemed to inspire her more than any therapist ever could!) We continued to make multiple trips a month to Rainbow for outpatient clinic visits where Colette's lab work and weight could be monitored. It was during these early weeks of February that we attempted a trial of full feeds by mouth only—no more tube feeds! Colette would still receive fluids and medications through the G-tube as she remained pretty obtuse when it came to the sippy cup; however, February 11th became Colette's first tube feed free day! Though she would occasionally require supplemental feeds through her G-tube, she would never again return to a full tube feed diet. Colette had reached another milestone!

Valentine's Day arrived (or "Loving Day" as TJ declared it) and was filled with hearts, balloons, and plenty of sugary treats.

February 14, 2019, Thursday

The past two days have been so beautiful—golden days—more exquisite because I know how swiftly all this beauty can vanish. I cherish these moments. I am memorizing the scenes, the words, the sensations. I look out my window, and I see the giant, soft falling snow I love so well. I look around me and see TJ's massive chocolate-colored eyes and Colette's face crinkled up in a smile. I hear TJ's endless chatter as he carries out imaginary conversations between little construction workers who are apparently planning a birthday party for Flossie that involves "rainbow popcorn," and I hear the clang of my nesting bowls as Colette scoots them around my kitchen floor. I'm like the Grinch saying, "Noise! Noise! Noise!" except instead of disgust, it is joy that fills me. These days are gifts, and I thank God for them.

I wrote the following about a week later after one of Colette's outpatient clinic visits.

February 20, 2019, Wednesday

I took both littles to Rainbow for Colette's check up today. We did beautifully! What a joy those two are! The staff is so wonderful to them both! They are showered with love…and Teddy Grahams.

The plan is for Colette to receive her fifth round of chemotherapy before an MRI and lumbar puncture on March 20th. Oh, how I am tempted to think, "It can't be bad—everything is so perfect now!" But I have learned not to be so foolish. We have (God-willing) one month. One month to savor every minute, and by God's grace we will do just that!

PS: TJ calls Colette's little pony tail a "unicorn horn."

As we entered the month of March, Colette seemed less like a "medically fragile" child then ever. She had begun cruising on furniture and was full of mischief! TJ had to learn to operate his world differently now that his sister was gaining grounds in the independence department; sharing had become a necessary means of survival. TJ was not the only one who had to alter his ways. I was reminded again that the best way to keep things safe was to keep them out of reach. A lesson beautifully illustrated by a particular pen and bed skirt that was destroyed by a very creative Colette who had managed to open a family size jar of vaseline and spread its contents all over the corner of my room. Colette was on the move!

During this time, Colette continued to be monitored for hearing loss due to the risks associated with the treatments she had received over the course of her life. Amazingly, these hearing tests showed no significant hearing loss as her growing vocabulary attested to. Our home was treated to the sweetest little voice and echoed with "Da-Lee!," "Ma-Ma!" and "Tee-JAY!"

Colette began her fifth round of chemotherapy in early March. The day of the MRI drew steadily nearer. A truth that could not be avoided however desperate we were to shrink from it.

March 12, 2019, Tuesday

The scan lurking in the future began its heavy assault on my emotions today. Up till now, I've been able to have a very textbook, theoretical view of things…It is a decision made by God. I can trust God. No need to fret. Move on with my day.

Today however, as I prepared Colette's chemotherapy while she sat in her high chair watching a nursery rhyme show, the reality of it all swept over me. Fear, desperation, and longing seemed to flow over every part of me like a tsunami wave crashing down over my carefully built theories. All I could do was beg God for help; the onslaught has continued all day.

Oh, please God have mercy, have compassion on me. Please, heal her—touch her, raise her up whole. Please don't let the cancer return.

This is the "pouring out of my heart" before Him [Psalm 62:8].

The following will be my attempt to encourage myself in the Lord. For I know You, God, to be the God of might and wonder. The God Who established this entire universe with its endless mysteries and wonders with the words of Your mouth. Your power and authority is boundless. You, God, can do whatever You desire. You require nothing. You depend on nothing. You are awesome in power and might.

Lord You are wise. You see not as man sees, but in one second You take in every bit of knowledge that ever was or ever will be. You see it all before You. You comprehend all things. You are not bound by time. You are God, all-knowing and all-wise.

Why this comforts me is the fact that You are GOOD. You love me. You see me here. Katie, the weak, the fearful. You have loved me. You have redeemed me. You have made me Your own. You know me completely, and You will not put me through one moment of unnecessary pain. If I feel anguish at Your hands it is because it is required to

159

bring about some great unfathomable good that I, with my finite mind, cannot foresee. Therefore, give me what I need. Give me faith to believe this. Faith to trust that what lies ahead will one day be understood and seen as good. Give me faith to trust You, to live each day from now till the 20th with a peace and joy that brings You glory.

The following day I wrote:

March 13, 2019, Wednesday

I feel so much better today. After I wrote last night, I read out of Jeremiah 42 where God tells the people, "Do not be afraid...of the things you are afraid of" [vs. 11]. It seems to me that following Christ is about learning not to fear what is terrifying. It is about having faith that all things are unfolding perfectly according to His perfect plan. We must relax in His capable hands. So that is what I'm doing. I am putting off fear and putting on faith.

The week before the scan was spent in doing just that, in battling fear and putting on faith. I worked to enjoy the moments that I had been given. On March 19th I wrote:

Here I am on the eve before another scan. Tomorrow I will read the title of the next chapter of the story God is writing for us. The Author is good. The Author is wise; therefore, the end of the story will be sweet and beautiful. I must not fear the next chapter. I must read, read, read, having faith that each chapter brings me closer to the sweetest and best of all endings.

A day later came these words:

March 20, 2019, Wednesday

BLISS! This next chapter God wrote appears to be titled BLISS! There is no tumor—all is well. What glorious words those are. How utterly relieved one feels to hear them. Praise God-NO TUMOR! Two more months! I pray the days are filled with gratitude, thanksgiving and growth. Please, Lord, bless these days You've given us. Use them to make us all more like You.

CHAPTER 16

Tiny Buds of Hope

With the glorious news of a clear scan, we danced through the final days of March—full of hope and bright plans for the days ahead. I remember now beginning to dream in earnest. Just as a person recovering from an injured limb first moves slowly, hesitantly, for fear of experiencing the pain that had for so long been associated with movement, so were my early attempts of dreaming. My hopes had been so often crushed that the hesitation to dream was very real. To lift up my eyes towards the future, to think beyond a two month increment, should I dare? Slowly, gingerly I began to do so, ever waiting for that expected blow. But it did not come. We now had three clean scans behind us. Would darkness ever come again?

On April 8th, Colette began her last round of chemotherapy. From this point on, it would merely be MRI scans at two months intervals until we hit the one year clean mark.

April 12, 2019, Friday I wrote:

Colette had her last chemotherapy treatment today! Oh, Praise God! What glorious bliss to push the flush through her G-tube and say like Poe's raven, "Nevermore!"

Oh, I could snuggle and kiss that girl to pieces—she is truly addicting. The more you watch her the more you want to watch her, those chubby arms (now in short sleeves that beautifully display her delicious rolls), that wild hair, the little kissable mouth. What a gift this time has been.

Picture: The kissable Colette at an outpatient clinic visit

During these days in April, Colette seemed to be yearning to hit that next milestone: walking. She was desperate to walk and would pretend to do so by holding on to any available hands and proudly marching around the

163

house. Her leg strength always seemed to last longer than her assistant's back strength, however, there were many willing to help her achieve her ambitious dreams.

Before long, Easter was upon us. An Easter so drastically different than the one a year before. How we praised God for His goodness to us! We spent the day celebrating Christ's resurrection and enjoying time with family. Colette particularly enjoyed her first Easter egg hunt in which every yellow egg was reserved for her, safe from the scavenging of her older, more active brother and cousins. These eggs were stuffed full with goldfish crackers, of which she certainly ate her body weight that day! How far she had come in one year!

The Monday after Easter found both TJ and Colette out of sorts. TJ was suffering from a cold, and though Colette had no upper respiratory symptoms, it was certain that she was not acting herself. The week continued in that fashion, and on April 25th I wrote:

My two little patients have been working to increase my patience! Colette is like a sticker—she just wants to cling to me! I'm getting even better at doing a day's work one handed as Colette rides on my hip wherever I go. If only I had a tail!

By my mom's birthday on April 30th, TJ had improved but Colette remained abnormally discontented and irritable for no apparent reason. Two days later, she began pulling at her head and ear. I called the oncology team who suggested that we take Colette for an evaluation at the pediatrician's office. Having examined Colette, the pediatrician decided to place her on antibiotics. The doctor saw no obvious signs of infection but thought Colette's irritability could possibly be from the start of an ear infection.

The last sentence in my journal that day was, "*Colette will go on the antibiotics and hopefully will return to her normal, happy self.*" How stinging the optimism is to me now.

CHAPTER 17

The Valley of the Shadow

ay 4, 2019, Saturday
M *These next pages will record the unfolding of a nightmare—yet one filtered through God's sovereign love. Truth, whether I can believe it or not.*

Colette did not return to her happy self yesterday. She was more inconsolable than ever, even with Tylenol and Motrin. I made multiple calls to the oncology clinic (all responded to by a nurse saying, "Keep calm, it is just an ear infection or teething"). Finally, I took Colette back to the pediatrician, begging God to give the doctor insight if something was truly wrong. At the doctor's office Colette became suddenly lethargic, which caused the pediatrician to agree with me that something more than an ear infection was going on. She sent us to Rainbow ER for an MRI.

It was there that we discovered the horrible truth. A T2 Turbo MRI revealed a new tumor, the size of a quarter in the center of Colette's brain. The tumor was blocking the drainage of the cerebrospinal fluid—causing the pain. Dr. Stearns was the one who gave us this news as (God ordained) he was on service and still at the hospital at that late hour. Dr. Tomei, who was on her way home, turned around to come back to the hospital to perform the emergency surgery to place an EVD [external ventricular drain] that would drain the fluid and relieve the built up pressure.

Per her norm, Colette left for the OR without a tear…I made up for her tears. She is now in PICU 15, extubated and happy, breaking our hearts through her unfathomable sweetness. I cannot write the plan tonight.

165

May 6, 2019, Monday

    Colette is now in the OR for the last time. She is having a shunt placed [a drain for cerebral spinal fluid that would go internally from her brain to her stomach, preventing the buildup of pressure and pain]. *Once she is recovered from the surgery, we will take her home. There is to be no more war, no more fighting. There will only be what is familiar, comforting and loving. I will be her hospital; by God's grace, I will be her hospice.*

    I am writing this by Wade Pond, the pool I have circled hundreds of times. Shadows of me surround this place. The ground here holds my tears. The water has borne witness to my pain, as for two years now I have come here to walk, cry and pray. It is the most beautiful, sunny, clear day—a beauty that reminds me that Colette is not to be pitied. What joy lays before her! She is robbed of nothing but pain, sorrow and agony. Praise God for such a hope—for such a future. It is just time that will separate us, for one day I will hold her again in His country where all will be safe. No threat, no fear, no thief lurking behind the next day. What a God—what a gift. Bless Him! Praise Him—how good!

    Last night was a treasure. Mom and I stayed with Colette in the PICU, and after a brief snooze from 7:00-9:30 PM, Colette was up and ready to party until 1:00 AM! We colored, made messes, ate snacks and snuggled. A slumber party with my daughter! <u>God is kind</u>.

May 7, 2019, Tuesday

    We are home…together. Colette's surgery went well. She had a rough afternoon but did better in the evening. She enjoyed another slumber party with her PICU nurse friends Sam and Elisse, and she even got her nails painted. After meeting with the social worker from hospice and Dr. Stearns this morning, we were able to take our little lady home. Praise God, what a gift! As soon as we got through the doors, Colette crawled straight to her walker and with wobbly, post-operative legs began pushing it around! What a darling! She played so contentedly…a beautiful day.

May 8, 2019, Wednesday

    Oh, my lovely Colette—how can you be so resilient and yet so vulnerable? Here she is two days after a brain surgery and on pain medications (which would make the average person groggy), playing like her old self—content and self-reliant as ever! She uses her walker to dominate the first floor, scoots my baking bowls around, throws her toy bugs and fills the house with her sweet voice crying "Da-Lee," "Ma-Ma!" and "A-men!" We played with Play-Doh and enjoyed the sunny (but cool) day by taking a stroll around the yard in the wagon. Her appetite is down, and she vomited once; but otherwise she seems happy and more than well-loved. How good God is to give us these days.

May 9, 2019, Thursday

Oh, how I wish they were wrong. She seems to be so full of life! She is <u>running</u> with her walker, turning corners and racing down the hall! She chatters away with her "dank-oo" and "Poppa" (always in a delicious whispery voice). It is so painful because I see all this, and in my heart, little seeds of hope begin to sprout. I don't water them. I don't nurture them yet still they grow. What if God does a miracle? What if He heals her? Oh, how I try to stomp out these little dreams because I know that the larger they grow the more pain they will produce when they are plucked up.

Let me just be thankful for this day…for every kiss, hug and squeeze. I am thankful for every time our eyes lock and my soul spasms with love and sorrow.

The weather was warm today so we went on a bike ride to the park this morning, early before anyone else had arrived. We had the park to ourselves and enjoyed the sun and wind. Colette loves the wind. She smiles and blinks as it blows into her sweet face.

It is evening now, and as the daylight disappears, my spirit sinks further and further. Evenings are terrible. Nights are almost unbearable.

May 10, 2019, Friday

God is teaching me the discipline of directing my mind. I am not at liberty to let my mind wander, to let thoughts flow freely. Every thought must be taken captive. Is it true, honest, just, pure, lovely, of good report, of any virtue [Phil. 4:8]?

I feel that this past week I have given myself the freedom to think and say and act however my heart led me. What a foolish way to live, now, more than ever.

God forgive me—for flailing about as if I have no Guide, no Comforter. Give me grace to be led and taught by You. Live through me, oh Man of Sorrows; for You are a God "Who is acquainted with grief." Teach me how to walk this road of darkness. Help me to endure just as You endured, because of the "joy set before me" [Heb. 12:2]. There <u>is</u> joy ahead. There is guaranteed happiness, peace and laughter ahead. I simply must endure by Your grace until then. God, help me.

This morning my parents, Kevin, Lyssa, Miller, Brynley and Kayla came over. The littles played their hearts out. Our visitors are few, and the time with them is limited. There is a mixture of sweetness and bitterness to them.

May 11, 2019, Saturday

I imagine in the future there will be many days like this—days I will be reluctant to record. Who wants to write: I watched my daughter all day…I gobbled up every sound she made, every fleeting expression, every particle of her sweet, beautiful frame. I drank it all in, and though it was sweet, it left me bitter. The more I drank, the more empty I felt. I love her more the further she inches away from me.

She slept more than usual today. I hate to admit it, to acknowledge it…but it is true. I will say no more about it. Tim's entire family came this evening. I'm glad they were able to see Colette, and yet there is such a sting in hearing voices, in seeing people buzz about and in watching others consumed with life. The sting radiates through my body because I am forced to watch the world move on. It is my life alone that has stopped. Occasionally, others stop too. They sigh and sympathize, but they all move on. Their bodies, minds and hearts move on; but I stay here. Forced to drink this bitter cup my Father has prepared for me.

Here comes the Great Comforter. Pages of bitterness and despair will not be met with silence…here comes Truth. This cup, this day, this Valley of the Shadow that looms before me—it has all been arranged for me by He who loves me best. He will not let me be swallowed up by sorrow. His grace will be enough, and in His presence, I will again find joy. Joy because He will receive Colette. Joy because He will care for me. She is going to His country where there are no tears; where <u>joy</u> is the "serious business" as C.S. Lewis says.

How bright and beautiful are her prospects! Blessed be our Great Saviour Who drank a bitter cup to make my bitterness sweet. Praise God.

May 13, 2019, Monday

Yesterday God gave me a wonderful Mother's Day. I just kept thinking that I am so full. God has stuffed into Colette's short life so many moments of closeness and connection. I am blessed because I have known since she was ten weeks old not to take one moment with her for granted. I have soaked her in, and I am full. What a gift!

Later

    Do you know that it is true—God is the "God of all comfort" [2 Cor. 1:3]. *He is "a very present help in trouble"* [Ps. 46:1].

    After putting TJ and Colette down for bed, my soul was sinking within me. The "night-time wolves" were circling; but I have learned their vulnerability: truth. In tears, I reminded myself of the truth.

    God loves me. He cares for me in my pain. I don't have to "earn" His favor. I don't have to be good enough for Him to have compassion on me. The Gospel has made me perfect and precious in His sight. I am secure in His love and care.

    God is sovereign. Nothing will occur tomorrow but by His command. Nothing. My future days are laid out for me minute by minute, according to His wise decree.

    God is being good. He only ever acts out of love for me. If it doesn't appear good, that is simply because He is not finished. I must have faith and keep moving forward, knowing one day I will see His goodness to me more clearly. I am in the midst of a process not at the end of it. I must, in faith, submit to pain for a time. Joy will come, but for now I must wait.

    Colette had a good day. Tomorrow's plan: snuggles.

    PS: The hospice nurse came to the house to check on Colette. She said Colette looks wonderful and wants us to keep her on the pain medicine every six hours to help alleviate any pain caused by the tumor as it grows.

May 14, 2019, Tuesday

    Today was difficult. Colette was increasingly irritable. I hate to acknowledge it; I hate to record it. It was a hard day. But there were still moments of joy. I had a lovely snuggle/walk with her in my arms, and she said "ice cream" and "ball" for the first time today.

    Giving pain medicine every four hours now.

May 15, 2019, Wednesday

    Colette is twenty-one months old today. For twenty-one months I have been able to glory in God's good gift to me. For twenty-one months I have been able to hold her, rock her, sing to her, pray for her and love her. Should this be her last month here on earth, it does not bring an end to the holding, rocking, singing, and praying. It will merely be a pause in them. They will be resumed one day and then continued eternally. Praise God, what a glorious truth. Thank You, God, for such a hope! As for loving her, that is something that began twenty-one months ago and will continue without the slightest of pauses, eternally.

    Happy twenty-one months blessed girl!

    As for the day, she did so much better. She was much more content and peaceful. Cinderella came to the house today (arranged by A Special Wish) to visit her and TJ, which was a treat. We attempted going to the park later in the day, but she did not enjoy it. We returned home so she could crawl and "walk" (holding my fingers). Much more fun!

May 16, 2019, Thursday

    I'm so "berry, berry" tired to quote TJ. We have had a day oozing with sweetness…an adventure day! A Special Wish arranged for us to have the Cleveland Children's Museum all to ourselves this morning! We got ready, packed and out the door by nine o'clock, full of excitement. The weather was just as glittery as our spirits—sunny, clear and bright. TJ and Colette (and Tim and I) had a blast at the museum. We packed in as much fun as we could before sweet, little Colette was too tired to keep going. She didn't fuss; she just laid her head on my shoulder and shut her eyes: the end!

    During the littles' naps, Tim and I worked in the yard. Everywhere I look outside I see beauty, and I have hope. Beauty is in store for Colette. One day we will enjoy it together.

    Dr. Stearns came to the house today and was happy with how Colette was doing. He thinks we should have good days and maybe even weeks yet.

May 17, 2019, Friday

    What is this peace that passes understanding? How is it my soul is full of joy? How can these things be? It has only been two weeks since the infliction of the greatest pain my heart has ever had to endure, and today I cannot explain the contentment, the calm, the joy. Who is like our God? Who can wrench from the jaws of the enemy and restore peace and hope? There is none like our God. It is true that "Earth has no sorrow that heaven cannot heal" *(Thomas Moore). Every day I see more clearly the beautiful hope. Colette's future is being molded by the hands of the God of Heaven, and I can be assured that her future will be good—whether by a miracle He gives her length of days on earth or whether by a miracle He takes her to paradise. It is His decision. I can just calmly watch. I can be still, cease striving, and watch my Father work. Thank you, God, for such hope, such peace, such joy. Being your daughter, what greater gift could I know. Blessed be Your name.*

May 18, 2019, Saturday

Once again that irrepressible little seedling called hope is sprouting up. Colette had another good day. She seems more and more herself. She did her walking while holding my fingers routine over and over! It seems to be her favorite pastime. She wants to walk by herself so badly!

May 19, 2019, Sunday

Colette continues to be all sunshine. So much sunshine, in fact, that she had a middle of the night spree. She got up around 3:00 AM crying her heart out; when I picked her up, she instantly began chatting. It was play time! She was such a character. Tim got up with us as well, and Colette just played and played. One thing she really enjoys is smashing things (and people) with a plastic golf club. She thoroughly enjoyed herself for about half an hour, then rubbed her eyes and began to cry. I put her back into her crib where she snuggled up with her unicorn Julia (who almost always ends up thrown out of the crib at some point during the night because I find her on the floor every morning...) and sailed into the Land of Nod.

It was in the 80s today and sunny, which allowed for a couple of stroller rides and a stop at the park.

May 20, 2019, Monday

We had a chilly day today. Such a contrast to the past two days. We were visited today by some of Colette's loyal PICU nurses, which was wonderful. Later, we took Colette to a local greenhouse to buy more plants for the garden—it was simply a lovely, sweet day. A day we could pretend all was normal.

May 21, 2019, Tuesday

Another chilly day. Poor TJ. He wakes up every morning with the question, "Is it hot outside yet?" He loves wearing shorts and "no coat!" What greater joy is there to a three-year-old?

171

As for the little sweet one, she had a more difficult day. She played but had more episodes of fussiness than normal. These episodes were resolved by extra pain medicine.

My mom came over later in the day and was delighted to discover that Colette has begun saying "Oh-MA!" We made book marks out of construction paper, and Colette semi-willingly finger painted them.

May 23, 2019, Thursday

Two years ago I searched the calendar wondering which day would be sanctified by Colette's birth. Which day would become sacred to my heart. How very different now to be looking and pondering which day will be sanctified by great sorrow. How can this be?

May 24, 2019, Friday

Yesterday was wonderful and awful all mixed together. The wonderful was so bright—and held such beauty. I saw a future of wholeness and joy for Colette; but the awful was so gruesomely dark. I saw that the days of feeling her warmth are slipping away.

She fits so perfectly in my arms. She reaches for me and up she comes, legs straddling my hip. My left arm and her right arm intertwined. We both know the routine, and we glide into position seamlessly. We are one entity. How much pain will it produce when we are torn apart!

My comfort is that it is a pain that I alone will have to bear. She, praise God, will experience nothing but joy. I am trying to forbid my mind from peering into the days ahead. I have learned that God gives no grace for the imagination. An imagined future is always harder to endure than the real thing, for reality is tempered with God's grace and presence.

Yesterday we made little lockets and keychains out of Colette's hair as well as a mold of her hand, which will certainly become a treasure.

May 25, 2019, Saturday

As I began to write, my curtains were drawn. Through a tiny slit between the curtain and the wall, I could see the trees I love so well dancing fiercely in the wind. I watched them for a while then reached to pull back the curtains to get a better view of their wild dance. But as I did, a thought flashed into my mind. This is like my view of Colette's future. I can see but a sliver of it; but what I can see tells me that it is something worth seeing, something magnificent. One day the curtain will be pulled back, and I will behold the beauty and wonder more fully. I need not fear what lies behind the curtain—the glimpse God has given me in the Bible is assurance enough—joy awaits.

Colette has had her typical day of chattering, "walking" via my assistance, and reading (and destroying) Pete the Cat books. She has gotten noticeably more irritable around the time her pain medicine is scheduled. She cries and lays her head on me. Once the medication is given, I carry her all over the house…walking, walking until the medicine starts to work and she is comfortable again.

May 26, 2019, Sunday

It appears we have come to the beginning of the end. Colette's eyes are now deviating to the left, and her strength and coordination are diminished. We had the nurse from hospice, Sam, come out first thing this morning; she started Colette on Ativan for agitation. The odd thing is that Colette will not sleep. We (by orders from Dr. Stearns) have increased her pain medicine dose and have added two sedative medications, and she has only slept an hour-and-a-half today. It is now almost 9:00 PM, and she has still not fallen asleep. I have walked and walked with her for hours. She is so tired. Her eyes are the saddest, most weary looking eyes; yet, no sleep.

My poor little girl, how can I help you?

Needless to say, this is a day of tears.

May 30, 2019, Thursday

The nightmare is upon us. That Sunday night, Tim and I tried everything to console Colette. I ended up pacing the floors with her—upstairs, downstairs and into the basement then back again. Hour upon hour, I carried her while Tim made repeated phone calls to nurses and Dr. Stearns who all worked to create a plan that would bring relief to Colette. Different medications were tried, but Colette was inconsolable.

Eventually we asked Kayla and my mom to come and help. At 11:45 Sunday night, the hospice nurse finally arrived. It was pitch black in the house—the darkness of night and the darkness of fear. She took one look, checked Colette's pupils and pulled up and administered Morphine. She said, "I'm giving this medicine to make her comfortable; she may pass at any minute. Her pupils are fixed. Her brain is herniating. She will pass in the next few minutes probably."

It has been four days since then. Colette is still with us. She is fading but still here, ashen, unconscious, but alive.

May 31, 2019, Friday

Colette is now victorious, by the mercy and grace of Jesus Christ. Praise God, it is finished.... all is well.

June 1, 2019, Saturday

Last June I wrote, "Welcome June! Oh, what high hopes I have for you!" I have no such hopes this year. I expect this June to be a bleak, dark June—what else could it be?

I have decided not to record the past week chronologically but simply to record what I feel like writing as I feel like writing.

After that awful moment last Sunday when the hospice nurse arrived and made her terrible declaration, I began to pace with Colette—the well-worn trail through the kitchen, dining room, living room and back. I clung to Colette until she slowly calmed in my arms. She was still breathing but was no longer responsive. I carried her upstairs to her room and began to rock her, covering her with a steady flow of tears of despair.

That Sunday night was a long, miserable night. Her room had never before held such anguish. I just cried—sometimes softly, sometimes heavily—the tears would not stop. Eventually the hospice nurse told us that Colette was stable for the moment, but her death was imminent, though perhaps hours away. She believed that the tumor had suddenly reached the point where it could grow no more without pushing the brain downwards, causing herniation. Colette would not recover.

As the night went on, Pastor Dunn came to pray; my mom, dad and sister came to give her a kiss goodbye. Each time someone turned to leave the room, my heart shattered anew. How could this be happening?

I thought of TJ, soundly sleeping in his room next door. I could not believe he would wake up to find his sister gone forever. But this was mercilessly not to be the case. Colette lived till the morning and several mornings after that.

I cannot write more about last week now. Today's sorrow is more than enough to battle. TJ came into our room around 7:30 this morning to announce, "It's morning time-

can you help me put my play clothes on?" I got him dressed for the day and endured the cutting questions about Colette. We talked about where she was and how we missed her.

"I miss her" seems too tame a phrase for the longing I feel. The feeling is much more fierce. It's a craving, aching, yearning, desperate reaching for the unreachable.

The funeral home director came this afternoon, and we finalized details.

Tuesday, 10:00-12:30 June 4th; service at 12:30.

Oh, how I dread it all. The quiet, the noise, the busyness, the solitude. It is all dreadful.

Oh, my girl—I miss you.

June 3, 2019, Monday

What a beautiful, clear, sunny day. A crystal, shimmery day. If this kind of beauty can be found on earth—what greatness is Colette experiencing in Heaven at this very moment?

Tim and I took TJ to the Metroparks. We stumbled across a lovely pond that housed one of my favorite birds, the heron, along with several chatty bullfrogs that made TJ chuckle every time they croaked. We visited the beautiful gardens and were chilled silent by the order and harmony of it all…roses, sky blue irises, a lily-pad covered pond with fountains. There was even a butterfly house.

I'm praying for tomorrow—praying that I think biblically. Colette is not there. Her body is not her. I will honor her body because it carried her; but she, my sweet, impish, courageous little girl, will be laughing and playing the entire time her body lies still and waiting. No need for tears! All is well. She is well.

I pray I will keep that mindset of truth.

Now to continue the tale…TJ and Colette.

175

The night before Colette's sudden decline (Sunday evening), TJ and I had a little talk as I was getting him ready for bed. TJ had seemed unsettled all day because of Colette's increased irritability. His poor world had gotten chaotic and disorganized again, and he wanted to know why. So as I tucked him into bed I told him that I would probably have to hold Colette a lot in the next few days because she was "cancer-sick" and would soon be going to live with Jesus in Heaven. His reply was to produce a pathetic cough and say "But I'm sick—you need to hold me." We had a brief chat about the difference between being "cancer sick" and "cough sick." I assured him that I would hold him as much as I could. Little did I know that the conversation would be the prelude to Colette's rapid deterioration.

I have already written about that horrible Sunday night so I will not revisit the details. I will only say how relieved I was when I saw the dark sky outside the nursery window starting to lighten…I knew morning was coming, and TJ would soon be awake. He would have a chance to see Colette one last time.

When I heard TJ's sweet chitter-chatter through the walls of the nursery, I sent Tim to go get him and to gently tell him what was going on (which was the counsel of the wonderful hospice nurse, Sam). TJ was too afraid to come in to see Colette that morning, but again, according to Sam's advice, we left the door to the nursery open while he played elsewhere in the house. As the day wore on, he gained more confidence and eventually came in. He had Flossie, his stuffed rabbit, give Colette a kiss, but by bedtime he was ready to give Colette a kiss himself.

As the days passed, he accepted Colette's stillness and "sleeping" appearance as the new normal. He had questions "Why is Colette still in her pjs?" "When will she wake up?" and, the one that seemed to trouble him the most, "When will she open her eyes?" He asked this multiple times to which I always answered, "When she goes to live with Jesus."

One day he surrounded Colette with her little plastic toy bugs that she loved so well and said, "When you open your eyes, you'll see Jesus; and you will have a bug on your head!" placing one final bug on her soft, still little head!

He laid by her, talked with us, and was simply with her. It was beautiful—her first little friend, her only little friend.

We had a beautiful salt lamp cross that was given to us by Mary, Colette's occupational therapist and friend. We left the light on the entire week. It glowed warmly and made the nights less grim. One day, when TJ was asking again about Colette's eyes opening, I responded as I always did, "They will open when she goes to see Jesus." To this, TJ said, "Oh, yes, she will go live with Jesus in there."(referring to the cross!)

He didn't see her much after she took a turn for the worse on Thursday, but that week held many sweet moments for the two of them. I pray daily now that it will not be their last sweet moments together but a foretaste of an eternity of closeness.

When TJ woke Friday morning, Colette was gone. He came into our room early and whispered, "Can you help me put my play clothes on?" I got up and followed him to his room.

While getting him dressed, I said, "TJ, Colette went to live with Jesus. Her eyes are open now!"

"They're open?!" he said.

"Yes!" I replied, and we both did a little happy cheer for our sweet girl whose eyes were finally open.

Later, as I prepared for the funeral, I looked back over my journals. I knew I could not trust myself to speak during the service; but I also knew that I could not remain silent. I could not let the moment pass. Though I had no faith in my own tongue, I decided I could have something read. I could let my words be spoken by the mouth of another. I searched through my journals—page after page of hope, love and fear. Then I found it, a journal entry written a year earlier after the completion of Colette's fifth and final round of chemotherapy. On that last night in the hospital I had written these words:

June 3, 2018, Sunday

Colette continues to make progress—so much so that we anticipate that she will go home tomorrow! It is ten weeks today since she left home...seven months since this journey began. Strangely, I feel overwhelmed with what is about to happen—terrified to shut the pages of this chapter in our lives. As horrible and painful as they were, they were still so precious—so filled with Colette. What will the next chapter hold? There is such an underlying fear—a nagging, thieving fear that refuses to let me rejoice with the others. A fear so terrifying that I cannot even write it. But I have learned in these past seven months, and here I go. I will take my mind and walk it through the paths of truth until it reaches the Rock that is higher than I.

God is Sovereign: He writes the script of my life. He alone dictates the next step. Chance doesn't have a say in what comes our way.

God is Good: His sovereign plan will be filtered through His infinite goodness. One day, I will look back and praise Him for every choice He made for me because I will see that it was good. If it is painful now, it means that the story is not over. I must keep going.

God is wise: He knows what the next step should be. If it doesn't appear to make sense, it is because His mind is infinite and mine is finite.

God is faithful. Never, ever, ever will I be alone. He will ever be at my side. The God of all-comfort, imminent, and omnipresent is loyal to me.

God's grace will always be enough. He will never let it be too much for me. <u>Do Not Fear The Future.</u>

I copied down these words with tears in my eyes—encouraged by the same truths that had lifted me up on that fearful night in the hospital a year earlier. When I was finished, I added the following:

June 3, 2019

In one year's time, that great fear that I could not look in the eyes has come. Colette is gone and my arms are empty.

But still, the path of truth beckons me—the path my feet know well, so often they have traveled it.

God is sovereign, so I am safe; God is good, so all is well, God is wise, so I need not fear; God is faithful, so I will not be alone.

True, the fear has come, but because of God, it fades away and peace will take its place.

These two entries would be read for me by my Pastor the next day, at Colette's funeral.

June 5, 2019, Wednesday

What bleak words to write: Colette's funeral is over. Misery to live, misery to recall, misery to record.

The church was full of those who loved her, prayed for her and fought for her; consequently, the church was full of broken hearts.

As for Colette, her sweet little body looked nothing like her! I almost smiled when I saw her. It was as if, without her spunky, courageous spirit, her body relaxed into a frozen slumber—still beautiful, but so unlike the <u>real</u> Colette. It made the parting easier—she was not there!

Dr. Stearns came—that wonderful, wonderful man—along with so many others from Rainbow: Dr. Casey, Liz, Allison, Noopur, Colleen, Hannah, Sam, Elisse, Jenn, people from Mac 6, people from the sedation unit, people from the outpatient clinic, even the president of Rainbow! Dr. Stearns told us that half of Rainbow tried to get off work today—how I love them all. How we fought!

We said our goodbyes, knowing that they would be just for a time. "That Day" is coming. All is well, and <u>all will be well.</u> What a good God He is to save us from our broken hearts! The death of infants is a result of the sin of mankind, a result of the curse, a result of being human. But the hope for infants—their salvation—is the result of mercy from a <u>very</u> good God.

We released a rainbow assortment of balloons at the cemetery. We hoped it would be a reminder in a place where we are tempted to look down, to instead look <u>UP</u>! Because He lives, she lives also…praise God, she lives.

God gave me an unbelievable peace and grace the entire day. So much so that it was not until I got home and tucked TJ into bed that I was able to sit down and let my heart break…..again. How can I resign myself to this? How can it be that only a month ago she was so well and now she is so permanently gone from this world? I cannot go on with this thought. I cannot, or I will shatter again. The truth is I must be resigned because the event has not occurred by mere chance. It has come because it has been ordered for me by my loving Father. So once more, <u>all is well, and all will be well.</u>

Picture: Colette the Victorious

CHAPTER 18

Victorious

I stand before a stone in a grassy field that reads:

Colette Diana Tomei Piazza
August 15, 2017-May 31, 2019

It has now been one year since Colette's passing. Beneath the inscription is the word *Victorious*. My eyes are drawn to that word. *Victorious*. I trace my fingers over the letters. *Victorious*. The incongruity is obvious. Here I stand, at the foot of a tiny grave. Here I stand, a mother with arms that are empty, and here I stand declaring victory. What has emptiness to do with victory?

How is loss linked to triumph?

The answer lies in a promise. A promise that I have had plenty of time to ponder throughout Colette's life. I have wondered over it during unending nights in the PICU; I have attempted to reason it out during long days of uncertainty. And a year ago I clung to this promise as Colette vanished from my life. This is the promise, my Father's promise, my claim to victory:

"Death is swallowed up in victory. Oh death, where is your sting? Oh, grave, where is your victory...thanks be to God, Who gives us the victory through our Lord Jesus Christ." (1 Cor. 15:54-57)

Death is swallowed up in victory. God promises victory. Through the redemptive work of Jesus, my Colette is alive. Though I cannot hear her voice, she is not silenced. Heaven rings with her laughter! Though I cannot touch her hands, they are not still! Her pain is over; her fight has ended. Her body, once marked by the scars of surgeries, is whole once more. No more cancer, no more chemotherapy, no more life-altering scans. No more fear, no more anxiety, no more sorrow. This is not mere wishful thinking; this is not fingers-crossed hoping. This is not something I tell myself to simply ease my pain. This is His promise. Once more, Jesus says,

"I am the resurrection, and the life: he Who believes in me, though he may die, yet shall he live." (John 11:25)

What a promise. What a victory. Colette is well and whole, and has an eternity before her to live! Endless days of joy have come; her sweet determination that was so evident in this life will carry on unchecked by pain or sorrow. That little face that would scrunch up into the most squishy smile will go on planting seeds of joy in all who meet her. What greater victory is there? Through the goodness of a merciful Savior, Colette is victorious.

And yet, I did not choose to mark her grave with the word *victorious* for this reason alone. Colette is not simply victorious in her death. She was victorious in her life. As I look back, I see her days on earth peppered with victories. Colette's twenty-one-and-a-half months of life had purpose and meaning. Things were accomplished through her life that could come about no other way. For truly, God never wastes pain. Not yours, not mine and certainly not a child's. She was the means of bringing people together, connecting hearts and lives, and inspiring people to hope. She made those who knew her stronger. She brought out resiliency, endurance and tenacity. She forced us to come face to face with our weaknesses, to humble ourselves before our God, to see our own frailty. She taught us to trust in God's goodness in spite of a seemingly lack of evidence of it. She pushed us to "walk by faith, not by sight" (2 Cor. 5:7). She did this in twenty-one-and-a-half months. She did this with a vocabulary of about eleven words. Her life and her suffering was not wasted:

"For God hath chosen the weak things of the world to confound the things which are mighty." (1 Cor. 1:27)

Her life on earth was victorious. The very fact that you are reading her story is evidence of her victory.

However, this book was not intended to merely tell of Colette's victory. She is not the only "weak thing" God has chosen to use to exhibit His might. This has been my story as well. I have shared with you my thoughts, my fears, my dreams as I traveled through the High Place and as I have carried a child through the Valley of the Shadow of Death. I have let you near so the true source of my victory can be seen.

I have often been told by those who know our story, "You are such a strong person." How I shudder when I hear those words! How I cringe to even record them! I have let you near to expose the truth: I am <u>not</u> a strong person; I have a strong God. It is through Christ that I did not slip during those days in the High Place; it is through Christ that I did not falter during the passage through the Valley of the Shadow of Death. It is through Christ that I have returned to the Land of the Living, and it is through Christ that I am filled now not only with peace but with joy. It is through Christ that I have been made "more than a conqueror" (Rom. 8:37). I have not only survived, I have flourished. I am richer for what I have lost. Yes, I grieve. Yes, I ache to have my daughter's sweet face nestled up against mine. I feel a sting every time I see a little dark-haired, dark-eyed girl. I hurt, but I am not broken.

I have learned to be content. I have learned to be patient. I have learned not to let a temporary loss rob me of present joy. I have learned to look to a hope beyond this life. I have been unfastened. Cut loose from the relentless desire to control and to manipulate my entire world in order to keep myself and those I love safe. I have learned to rest in the goodness of an unceasingly good God.

I have an unquenchable joy. I have an unshakeable peace. I have an unstoppable hope. Through Christ I am victorious.

CHAPTER 19

The Path to Victory

I cannot conclude without speaking to you personally as a reader. You have invested your time and your emotional energy to read our story, to share in our suffering and to watch us gain the victory. You have given us the gift of your attention. I cannot close without reaching out to you: how are you? I am not asking at a surface level. I am not waiting to hear the obligatory "fine" or "great!" I am asking you to pause and be still. How are you? How is your soul? The spirit within you? Are you a victor, headed to victory? Do you have a deep, unshakeable peace within you? Or do you feel your uncertainty, fear and anxiety grow the longer you sit in silence? Please, hear me—it does not have to be that way. Please, let me show you the path to victory; let me lead you to the One Who said,

"In Me you may have peace. In the world, you will have tribulation. But take heart; I have overcome the world." (John 16:33 ESV)

Let me present to you Jesus.

The Bible speaks of the dis-ease found in the soul of every person. That nagging feeling that surfaces in the random moments of life that says, "All is not well." It comes in moments of heartache and sorrow. The spirit within you cries out, "This is not how life should be!" It comes even in moments of great success; or, more accurately, it comes just following moments of great success. As the dust settles and the sparkle vanishes, the soul within you whispers, "I thought I would feel better when I achieved this…" There

184

is an unrest, an emptiness that permeates all life. You think, if I just go faster, work harder, reach further—I can extinguish it. But the moment you stop, the emptiness returns. There is no escaping it. The Bible devotes the entire book of Ecclesiastes to this pervasive emptiness saying in one passage,

"For what has man for all his labor, and for the striving of his heart with which he has toiled under the sun? For all his days are sorrowful, and his work burdensome; even in the night his heart takes no rest. This also is vanity." (Ecc. 2:23-24)

You want something more; you crave something more. The Bible says this is because you were made for something more. You were made to have peace with God. You were made to know and be known by Him. You were made to be His child. But this is where the problem lies. God is holy. He is morally perfect in all His ways. To have peace with God, you must be morally perfect as well. Not "good enough" or "mostly good," you must be perfect. Peace with God requires nothing less.

"But that is not possible!" you object, and you are absolutely right. There is not a person on earth who can achieve this perfection. The Bible recognizes this problem saying,

"There is none righteous; no, not one." (Rom. 3:10)

The problem grows deeper because not only do we lack the moral perfection that is required for peace with God, but our sinfulness creates a wedge that must be dealt with. Our sin must be paid for. The Bible speaks of this saying in Romans, "The wages [or consequence] of sin is death." (Rom. 6:23)

The situation would be hopeless except for the fact that God is not only holy, He is merciful. He has taken compassion on us and has provided a way to offer us peace not through our own efforts but through the work of His Son Jesus. The Bible describes it this way,

"But now in Christ Jesus you who once were far off have been brought near by the blood of Christ. For He Himself is our peace, who has made us both one and has broken down in His flesh the dividing wall of hostility...[so that He might] reconcile us both to God in one body through the cross, thereby killing the hostility."(Eph. 2:13-16)

Jesus came to the world, lived a sinless life, died on the cross and rose again from the dead three days later. This is God's plan for peace. You see, by Jesus living a perfect life He produced the moral perfection we could not achieve on our own. His death on the cross paid for the sin we could not pay for on our own. He created an opportunity for peace between God and man. Jesus said of Himself,

"I am the way, the truth, and the life. No one comes to the Father [God] except through me." (John 14:6)

Jesus is the path to peace; He is the path to victory. He offers to you,

"Come unto me, all you who labor and are heavy laden, and I will give you rest." (Matt. 11:28)

He reaches out to you. All that stands between you and that peace your soul so desperately craves is you. This very moment, turn from your own way. Give up the idea of earning peace with God. Give up the attempt of seeking satisfaction elsewhere. Put your faith in the finished work of Jesus Christ. Ask Him to forgive your sin, to give you His perfection and to become your Savior. In Him, you will find peace; through Him, you can say, "All is well, and all will be well."

The path to peace beckons, beyond it lies victory.

APPENDIX A

Normal Vital Signs for a 6-12 month old:

(PALS Algorithms 2020)

Pulse/Heart Rate: 90-160

Respirations: 22-38

Blood Pressure: 80-100/55-65

Pulse Oximetry: 94-100%

ABOUT AUTHOR

KATIE PIAZZA is an emergency room nurse with a B.A. in psychology. She is pursuing certification as a biblical counselor through the Association of Certified Biblical Counselors (ACBC). She has a passion for helping others see God's abundant love and goodness, starting with those within her own home. She lives in Avon, Ohio, with her husband and two boys and is an avid reader and writer.

ABOUT KHARIS PUBLISHING

Kharis Publishing, an imprint of Kharis Media LLC, is a leading inspirational and faith publisher with a core mission to publish impactful books, and support at-risk children with literacy tools.

Kharis Publishing is an independent, traditional publishing house committed to the dual mission of giving voice to under-represented writers, and equipping orphans with literacy too. Therefore, the publisher channels a portion of proceeds into establishing mini-libraries or resource centers for orphanages in developing countries, so these kids will learn to read, dream, and grow. Every time you purchase a book from Kharis Publishing or partner as an author, you are helping give these kids an amazing opportunity to read, dream, and grow. Kharis Publishing is an imprint of Kharis Media LLC. Learn more at https://www.kharispublishing.com

"Thanks be to God,

who gives us the victory

through our Lord Jesus Christ."

(1 Corinthians 15: 57, NASB)

Victorious

Victorious

CPSIA information can be obtained
at www.ICGtesting.com
Printed in the USA
FSHW021129051020

9 781946 277695